Jazzy Vegetarian

LIVELY VEGAN CUISINE THAT'S EASY AND DELICIOUS

Laura Theodore

BOOK PUBLISHING COMPANY
Summertown, Tennessee

Library of Congress Cataloging-in-Publication Data

Theodore, Laura.
    Jazzy vegetarian : lively vegan cuisine that's easy and delicious / Laura Theodore.
        p. cm.
    Includes index.
    ISBN 978-1-57067-261-3 (hardcover) — ISBN 978-1-57067-946-9 (e-book)
    1. Vegan cooking.   2. Vegans.   I. Title.
    TX837.T456 2011
    641.5'636—dc23
                                                    2011032531

Front and back cover photos: Joe Orecchio
Interior photos: Andy Ebberbach, Warren Jefferson
Hair and makeup: Christina Turino
Cover and interior design: John Wincek

Book Publishing Company
P.O. Box 99
Summertown, TN 38483
888-260-8458
www.bookpubco.com

ISBN: 978-1-57067-261-3

Printed in the United States of America

17 16 15 14 13 12 11   9 8 7 6 5 4 3 2 1

Book Publishing Company is a member of Green Press Initiative. We chose to print this title on paper with 100% postconsumer recycled content, processed without chlorine, which saves the following natural resources:

47 trees
1,374 pounds of solid waste
21,681 gallons of water
4,808 pounds of greenhouse gases
19 million BTU of energy

For more information on Green Press Initiative, visit www.greenpressinitiative.org.

Environmental impact estimates were made using the Environmental Defense Fund Paper Calculator. For more information visit www.papercalculator.org.

Printed on recycled paper.

BOOK PUBLISHING COMPANY

green press INITIATIVE

"Nothing will benefit human health
and increase chances for
survival of life on Earth
as much as the evolution to
a vegetarian diet."

ALBERT EINSTEIN

Chocolate Chip-Banana Muffins, page 53

Contents

Jazzy Vegetarian Not Liver, page 61

Foreword

There are few people who disagree with the idea that eating a better diet is the key to enjoying better health, and an increasing body of medical evidence shows that many degenerative diseases can be stopped and even reversed by eating the right diet: one based on whole plant foods. I've been writing and lecturing on this topic for the last fifteen years.

Unfortunately, one of the impediments to dietary change for many people continues to be the fear that food will no longer be enjoyable—that one must choose between delicious food or nutritious food, and that dishes certainly can't be both. The myth prevails that people who practice dietary excellence must be living on tree bark and pine cones!

Laura Theodore has created a book that offers dishes that are both mouthwatering and healthful while also being accessible even to those who are not experienced cooks. This book is a great resource not only for people who are just beginning their journey toward health-promoting eating, but also for those of us who are already committed to eating a plant-based diet and are looking for new food ideas and cooking adventures.

The solution to the health-care crisis in the United States is not to be found in new drugs and medical procedures, but rather in teaching people to improve their health through adopting a whole-foods, plant-based diet. While many people know what they are not supposed to eat, few know what to eat instead. *Jazzy Vegetarian* reaches out to people, regardless of their current dietary patterns, takes them by the hand, and helps them transition to plant-based eating enjoyably and effortlessly. I wish this book had been available when I was improving my own family's diet many years ago!

Pamela A. Popper, PhD, ND
Featured expert in the acclaimed documentary *Forks Over Knives*
President, the Wellness Forum, Columbus, Ohio

Jazzy Vegetarian gratefully acknowledges our sponsors, Tropicana and Quaker, whose generous support has made it possible to share these recipes with the world.

Acknowledgments

There are so many incredible people to thank. First and foremost, I'd like to thank Andy, my loving, caring husband of twenty-one years, who has ceaselessly supported me on this exciting journey. He has eagerly been my chief taste tester for all of the recipes in this book and so many more.

I would like to express my heartfelt gratitude to my family and friends. They have been a continual source of unconditional love and gracious support of my life path and have lent their willing—and pleased—palates to my experiments in plant-based cuisine. I have been blessed to learn so much about cooking from my mother, Marilou; my grandmothers, Dot and Ann; my stepmother, Chris; and my mother-in-law, Anita. Many of the creations in this book are based on their traditional recipes, some of them passed down for generations, inspiring me to create plant-based recipes with those classic flavors in mind. I am thankful to my sister, Julie, for her faithful support and helpful recipe ideas, and to my step-sisters, Wendy, Karla, and Shelly, for our discussions about creating healthful dishes.

My deep appreciation goes to Regina Eisenberg, Dave Davis, Cheri Arbini, Pat Kruis, Dr. Pam Popper, Ginny Shea, Peter Capozzi, and John Capozzi. This project would not have been possible without their talent, guidance, hard work, and continued support.

I'm grateful to all of the fabulous folks at Book Publishing Company: Cynthia Holzapfel, for her vision and patience in shepherding this book through the publishing process; my editors, Jo Stepaniak and Jasmine Star, for their skill, perception, and attention to detail; and Bob Holzapfel, Mary Ellen Bowen, Rick Diamond, Warren Jefferson, and Alan Roettinger, for their assistance and input.

I also extend a heartfelt thank-you to Garrison Botts for his caring advice and support of both my cooking and musical careers; to my longtime friend Dr. Jonny Bowden for his continued enthusiastic and supportive spirit; to Cherry Huntoon and all of the great folks at Kings Cooking Studio for believing in the Jazzy Vegetarian concept; and all of the wonderful, insightful guests who have taken the time to share their expertise on my weekly radio show, as well as the hardworking farmers I've been fortunate to meet and learn from.

Many of these recipes were inspired by chatting, dining, and cooking with my beautiful, talented, and incredible girlfriends. Much love and many thanks go to Debby, Lili, Sara, Chrissy, Maria, Renee, Kit, Carolyn, Lillian, Kathy, and Suzanne for their constant support. I also thank my darling goddaughter, Katherine, for her love—and for loving my cooking!

Thanks to Marcy Baskin, who introduced me to the wonderful world of vegetarian cooking thirty-five years ago. I also owe a debt of gratitude to the vegan and vegetarian cookbook authors, nutritionists, and physicians who have shared their thoughts and ideas with me throughout the years.

These acknowledgments wouldn't be complete without a thank-you to the animals. This cookbook is for them.

Jazzy Vegetarian

LIVELY VEGAN CUISINE THAT'S EASY AND DELICIOUS

Jazzy Vegetarian

Hosted by
Laura Theodore

Introduction

MY JOURNEY FROM JAZZ SINGER TO PROMOTER OF VEGAN FOOD

Seeking to live a vegan lifestyle has been an inspiring and gratifying journey for me. Many people ask how I went from being a jazz singer to promoting vegan food. The best way to answer that question lies in the name I chose to represent where I am today: the Jazzy Vegetarian.

I originally became interested in plant-based cooking many years ago when, as an aspiring jazz singer, I moved to the Boston area to study music. That's where I first encountered a local "health food store." Back then, natural food stores weren't the upscale wonders of today. Often they felt more like rustic barns with barrels of brown rice, other grains, and an assortment of flours, and a few shelves sparsely stocked with hand-packed bags of nuts and dried fruits and some basic packaged goods.

My friend Marcy worked at that Boston health food store and had just penned a vegetarian cookbook—a forty-page booklet that sold for just two dollars. Though modest, it was chock-full of innovative recipes, ingredients, and ideas. Because of my lifelong love for animals, I was intrigued by Marcy's culinary outlook and began experimenting with converting my cherished family recipes into tasty vegetarian versions.

Eventually I moved to New York City, married, and carved my path as a jazz singer and actor—and also completely eliminated meat from my diet. Then I started to experiment with removing eggs and dairy products

too. Because I loved having groups of friends over for dinner parties and for the holidays, I began to focus on creating enticing plant-based dishes that would appeal to everyone, even those who weren't vegans or even vegetarians. As my culinary creations became increasingly popular with our New York crowd, I started writing down the recipes that were hits at the various soirees so often held in our small New York apartment.

After twenty years of city life, we decided to move to a more suburban atmosphere, making a welcome transition from a crowded apartment in the noisy city to a home surrounded by the sounds of rustling trees and busy birds. I found myself with a larger kitchen to cook in, but I no longer had easy access to many of the ingredients that had been so readily available in the Big Apple. So my vegan voyage continued with new challenges. I began adapting my recipes, fine-tuning them to utilize ingredients I could easily obtain locally while still producing fabulous vegan fare that would please the omnivorous palates of our new neighbors, overnight guests from the city, and visiting relatives.

This is the point when it all came together for me and the Jazzy Vegetarian was born. Living the vegan lifestyle and sharing it with friends and family had moved to center stage. Creating appetizing, delicious, and nutritious recipes and offering tips for living a more compassionate lifestyle have become my focus. Beyond this book, my endeavors in this area include a weekly radio show (*Jazzy Vegetarian Radio*), a website (jazzyvegetarian.com), and a nationally televised cooking show on public television (*Jazzy Vegetarian*), not to mention a blog and frequent updates on Twitter. Through all of these means, my goal is to help people who want to incorporate more vegan meals into their everyday lives but don't know where to begin. The delightfully delicious recipes you'll find in this book are the perfect way to introduce plant-based meals to anyone and everyone and to make the move from omnivore to full-time vegan a pleasant and rewarding journey.

Embracing a Plant-Based Lifestyle

I have a motto: "Making the world a better place, one recipe at a time." If you're new to the advantages of a plant-based diet, that may seem a bit nonsensical. How can a recipe make the world a better place? Yet when you consider the many reasons why people embrace a plant-based diet, such as showing compassion for animals, seeking better health, and striving to be more environmentally responsible, the benefits are clear. Whatever your reasons may be for exploring the recipes in this book, I thank you for joining me in my effort to make the world a better place!

Within these pages you'll find recipes that speak to you and your lifestyle, whether you are simply looking to add a few plant-based dishes to your menus or are a dedicated vegan. And there it is: that word "vegan." Part of my mission is to erase any stigma you may associate with it. There seems to be much confusion around the word "vegan," and you may wonder what it really means. The way I see it, a vegan is someone who eats a purely plant-based diet of fruits, vegetables, grains, legumes, nuts, and seeds and avoids meat, poultry, seafood, eggs, and dairy products.

"Making the world a better place, one recipe at a time."

LAURA THEODORE, THE JAZZY VEGETARIAN

So the operative term is "plant-based," and that might be a more user-friendly way to describe the recipes in this book. Who doesn't love plants? They transform the warmth of the sun and the rich soil of the earth into endless forms that grace our tables and also offer a visual feast, from dazzling floral displays to expansive fields of wheat swaying in the wind. So rather than focusing on the restrictions of a vegan diet, think instead of *expanding* your diet to include more plant-based meals.

When contemplating the transition, many people ask, "What will I eat if I don't eat meat, milk, or eggs?" or "Where will I buy my food?" The truth is, all the ingredients you need to make the recipes in this book can be found at any well-stocked supermarket, and as you'll see, many of the recipes in this book emulate traditional favorites. Plus, most of the recipes are easy to prepare and don't require that you spend hours in the kitchen. In fact, I came up with most of the dishes in this book when I was short on time but wanted to create a tasty meal from scratch using whatever ingredients I had on hand. Like most people in this modern world, I often find that there aren't enough hours in the day. As a result, I've developed many kitchen shortcuts over the years, and I'm excited to share them with you.

My philosophy about quick and healthful home cooking is that it isn't rocket science. I've done the groundwork for you, coming up with plant-based dishes that are both delicious and nutritious. If you have questions about specific ingredients or what to seek out when shopping, take a look at chapter 1. If you're at a loss as to how to put together a well-rounded vegan meal, chapter 2 is for you. It offers guidance on menu planning, along with twelve specific menus using the recipes in this book, tailored to different occasions. Once you become familiar with this way of cooking, I encourage you to jazz it up, improvising with your favorite ingredients or whatever is in season to create your own taste sensations.

From festive lasagna and stuffed vegetables to hearty soups and chilis to rich and decadent desserts, this book offers a wide range of recipes, and I'm confident that within these pages you'll find dishes that you and yours will truly love to eat. And best of all, you'll be making the world a better place, one tasty recipe at a time. Enjoy!

The Basics

I find certain ingredients and information to be essential in my daily cooking. I discuss them in this chapter to help you get more familiar with ingredients I call for often, and in the hopes of making your kitchen endeavors easier, more efficient, and more enjoyable.

Glossary of Ingredients

In developing the recipes for this cookbook, one of my goals was to focus on using ingredients that are readily available in any well-stocked supermarket. You're probably familiar with most of the ingredients I call for, but a few are worth discussing, either because they're somewhat unusual or because I'd like to give you some pointers or helpful information about them. As you'll see, I often have recommendations for the types of products to buy. I believe this is a big part of making the world a better place, one recipe at a time!

I'll also take this opportunity to address a couple of overarching issues. First, I recommend that you buy organically grown ingredients and products whenever possible. Some of the reasons for doing so are precisely the same as for choosing a plant-based diet: organic growing methods are easier on the planet, and because organic agriculture doesn't carry the toxic burden of conventional methods, organic products are more healthful—for you and those you love, for the environment at large, and for all of the earth's creatures, who depend on clean soil, air, and water to thrive. Organic products may be a bit more expensive, but purchase them when you can and look at it as an investment in your health and the future of the planet.

I also recommend that you steer clear of genetically modified (GM) ingredients and products that use these ingredients, if for no other reason than that we don't know the long-term impacts of this technology. One thing we do know, however, is that engineered genes can spread from commercially cultivated crops into non-GM crops and even into other species—and possibly humans. It simply isn't worth the risk. Unfortunately, the United States and Canada don't require that GM products be labeled as such. However, they also don't allow GM foods to be labeled as 100 percent organic. So buying organic products is one way to ensure that you aren't purchasing foods that are intentionally genetically modified. Because soybeans, corn, and canola are among the crops most likely to be genetically modified, purchasing organic is especially important with these. That includes all soy foods, such as tofu, tempeh, miso, and tamari.

Having considered those unfortunate realities, let's get down to the fun part: obtaining the ingredients you actually want to cook with! If your grocer currently doesn't carry an item you're looking for, ask the store manager to order the item for you. More often than not, this simple tactic works, and it may even lead to that product being regularly stocked and available to the entire community. When you make your request, you might emphasize that others would also be interested in purchasing the product. For example, a few years ago, I couldn't find quinoa at one of my local markets. When I asked the manager to stock it, he looked at me quizzically and asked what quinoa was. After describing quinoa, I explained that there was a growing interest in cooking with this versatile and highly nutritious grain, perhaps making it lucrative for the store to carry it on a regular basis. The next time I shopped there, I was pleasantly surprised to find quinoa offered next to the rice. To this day, that market still carries quinoa.

Brown sugar. Brown sugar is simply white sugar with molasses mixed in, giving it a rich, distinctive flavor. Given how it's made, it presents the same quandary for vegans that white sugar does: when white sugar is made from sugarcane, the filtration process sometimes utilizes bone char. If this concerns you, look for brown sugar labeled as vegan. Perhaps the more weighty issues are the intensive agricultural methods used for conventionally grown sugarcane or sugar beets and the treatment of fieldworkers.

Given this state of affairs, I recommend that you opt for organic fair-trade sugar whenever possible. Chances are, those brands will also be vegan.

Cheese, vegan. There are many tasty nondairy cheeses made from almonds, rice, soy, arrowroot, pea protein, or tapioca starch, and even hempseeds in the marketplace these days. They come in a variety of flavors, and most of them melt better than earlier versions, so you can typically substitute vegan cheese for dairy cheese in recipes. When purchasing vegan cheese, be sure it's free of casein or calcium caseinate, milk proteins that may be used for texture.

Cocoa powder, unsweetened. Cocoa powder is made by grinding cacao beans and pressing out the cocoa butter, resulting in a dense powder that's low in fat but high in flavor. Because cacao agriculture has an especially poor track record on human rights and child labor, buy fair-trade cocoa powder whenever possible. Chances are, it will also be organic.

Dark chocolate, vegan. The highest-quality dark chocolate is made by adding only sugar and fat (typically cocoa butter) to ground cacao beans, the seeds from cacao (chocolate) trees, so it's typically vegan, but do read the label to be sure. For the same reasons discussed for brown sugar and cocoa powder, try to purchase fair-trade, organic chocolate. For maximum flavor, I recommend opting for chocolate with at least 60 percent cacao content.

Extra-virgin olive oil. Olive oil is a rich and flavorful fruit oil obtained from olives. The International Olive Oil Council defines extra-virgin olive oil as being produced by cold pressing the olives, containing no more than 0.8 percent acidity, and having a superior flavor. This delectable oil is delicious in salad dressings, as a dip for crusty bread, and for use in sautéing.

Flaxseed oil. Derived from the seeds of the flax plant, flaxseed oil is less stable than many other oils, so it shouldn't be heated or used for cooking. Look for flaxseed oil in the refrigerated section of your natural food store and put it in your refrigerator once you arrive home. Be sure to use it up by the expiration date stamped on the bottle. Flaxseed oil has a distinct but delicate taste. A great way to begin to incorporate flaxseed oil into your diet is to use two parts olive oil to one part flaxseed oil when making salad dressings.

Maple syrup. Buy organic maple syrup whenever possible to avoid undesirable additives and to support healthy forests. I like to cook with Grade B maple syrup, which has a darker color and thicker consistency than Grade A, because it imparts a denser maple flavor to the finished dish or baked good. If you prefer a more subtle maple taste, use the Grade A variety.

Margarine, vegan. Vegan margarine can be substituted for butter or other margarines in any recipe. Look for a brand that's free of hydrogenated oils, which are known to have serious adverse health effects. Because oils (which are used to make margarine) are a concentrated product, they tend to contain higher levels of any toxins or pesticide residues, so it's especially important to use margarine made from organic oil. This also helps ensure it's free of genetically modified ingredients.

Marinara sauce. Using a good-quality jarred marinara sauce is a real time-saver for recipes such as lasagna, chili, casseroles, stews, and more. I recommend that you keep several jars of marinara sauce in your pantry at all times; they'll come in handy for last-minute meals or whenever time is at a premium. Opt for jarred rather than canned marinara to avoid a metallic taste and read the label to make sure it doesn't include dairy or meat products.

Mayonnaise, vegan. Egg-free vegan mayonnaise can be used in place of traditional mayonnaise in almost any recipe. It is often but not always soy based. Available at natural food stores and many supermarkets, it is usually stocked in either the refrigerated section or the condiment aisle. Try several brands to discover your favorite.

Meat analogs. Meat analogs, usually made from wheat gluten or soy, are great to use if you want a meaty texture, flavor, or appearance, especially in lasagna, pasta dishes, chili, stir-fries, or sandwiches. You may find them helpful if you are transitioning from a meat-based diet or are cooking for nonvegetarians. They come in a wide variety of forms: veggie burgers, sausages, and deli slices. There even are products that emulate ground round, canadian bacon, and pepperoni. You can easily find these faux meats at natural food stores and most well-stocked supermarkets.

Miso. A culinary staple in Japan, miso is a thick, salty, fermented paste made with soybeans, sometimes in combination with other beans, grains, or additional ingredients. It can be used to enhance the flavor of dips, sauces, soups, spreads, stews, and more. I typically use white miso, which has a delicate flavor and is less salty; however, any variety of light miso is fine for the recipes in this book. When adding miso to hot foods, stir it into the food just before serving, as high heat destroys its beneficial enzymes. To help distribute the miso evenly, mix it into a bit of warm water or broth before adding it to the dish.

Nondairy milk. Nondairy milk, once relegated to the shelves of natural foods stores, is now available in most supermarkets. You'll find a number of varieties beyond soymilk, made with almonds, coconut, hazelnuts, hempseeds, oats, or rice, and unsweetened, plain, and flavored versions. Choose unsweetened, plain nondairy milk for savory recipes. The flavored and sweetened varieties are ideal for smoothies, baking, pouring over cereal, or just plain sipping.

Quinoa. This excellent alternative to brown rice is technically the seed of an herbaceous flowering plant, not a cereal grass, but its texture, flavor, and uses echo those of many true grains, so it's generally thought of as a grain. It's quick to prepare, cooking up in about fifteen minutes. In addition to being high in protein, quinoa contains all eight essential amino acids in balanced proportions, making it one of the few plant sources of complete protein. It's delightful alongside a generous serving of steamed vegetables or cooked up with canned beans to make a quick and hearty supper. It also works well as a delicious hot breakfast porridge.

Salsa. There are many varieties of jarred salsa available in most supermarkets, in a range of flavors from mild and sweet to hot and spicy. In addition to the more typical tomato salsa, experiment with salsas based on other vegetables or even fruits. Some tasty alternatives include mango, pineapple, and chipotle. As with marinara sauce, keep several jars of salsa stocked in your pantry to enhance chilis and soups or use as a quick topping for baked potatoes. Or simply pour some salsa into a bowl and serve it with tortilla chips, veggie sticks, or other dippers.

Tamari, reduced-sodium. Tamari is soy sauce that's fermented naturally, rather than being produced by an industrial hydrolysis process as conventional soy sauce is. As a result, its flavor is both more complex and more subtle than that of conventional soy sauce. The reduced-sodium version has about 25 percent less sodium than standard tamari, helping to reduce the sodium in your recipes while providing more flavor enhancement than table salt. When cooking, you can replace every ¼ teaspoon of sea salt (which contains about 580 milligrams of sodium) with 1 teaspoon of reduced-sodium tamari (which contains only about 230 milligrams of sodium). Make sure to buy tamari that has been made with GM-free soybeans and that doesn't include MSG or artificial preservatives. Use it as a flavor booster in sauces and vegan gravies or in marinades for tofu, tempeh, mushrooms, and winter squash. It's also a great way to subtly enhance the flavor of stir-fries, steamed vegetables, pasta dishes, soups, and just about any savory dish.

Tempeh. Tempeh is made by fermenting soybeans, sometimes in combination with other ingredients, such as legumes and grains. Like tofu it has a high protein content and is a complete protein, and it also absorbs marinades beautifully. However, it has more character than tofu, including a mild mushroomlike flavor and a slightly chewy texture, making it an ideal meat substitute. It must be cooked before eating and takes well to a wide variety of cooking methods: baking, grilling, steaming, stir-frying, and more. As with all soy products, purchase tempeh that's labeled organic or non-GM. Once you get familiar with tempeh, I'm sure you'll want to cook with it on a regular basis.

Tofu. A mainstay in vegetarian diets and a great source of high-quality protein, tofu is made from soybeans, water, and a coagulant. It's a versatile ingredient that works well in everything from casseroles and stir-fries to puddings and smoothies. It can also be used as a substitute for ricotta or cottage cheese in dishes like lasagna and vegetable casseroles. Plain tofu is widely available and comes in two main forms: regular (packed in water and refrigerated) and silken (in aseptic cartons and refrigerated tubs). Each type is available in soft, firm, and extra-firm varieties. You can also purchase baked tofu in a variety of flavors, including hickory-smoked, italian, lemon pepper, and various Asian-inspired flavors.

Vegetable broth and bouillon cubes. Most supermarkets carry organic vegetable broth packaged in aseptic cartons. Keep several in your pantry to enhance soups, stews, chilis, sauces, and casseroles. Vegetable bouillon cubes are handy to use in the same way. Cubes are convenient to use as a last-minute flavor enhancer because they can just be crumbled into soups, sauces, and gravies. Make sure to buy bouillon cubes that don't contain hydrogenated oils, and, as always, organic is a plus.

Vegetable oil. Some of the recipes in this book call for vegetable oil. When you see this listed as an ingredient, almost any vegetable oil will do. While unrefined oils may seem like the best bet because they are less intensively processed, many of them are easily damaged by heat. Unrefined olive, sesame, and peanut oils can take more heat (up to 350 degrees F) than other unrefined oils. For higher heat cooking, consider high-oleic safflower or sunflower oil.

Water. If, like most folks, you get your tap water from a municipal water system, I encourage you to filter all of the water you use for cooking and drinking. A countertop water filter is a modest investment that will repay you a thousandfold in tastier, more healthful water. It's especially important to use filtered water or springwater in teas, smoothies, and other beverages so their delicate flavors aren't compromised.

Wheat germ. Wheat germ, the embryo of the wheat kernel, is dense in flavor, texture, and nutrients, especially protein, B vitamins, and healthful fats. It should be refrigerated after opening to prevent it from becoming rancid. Wheat germ is available in supermarkets and natural food stores in both raw and toasted forms. Most of the recipes in this book call for toasted wheat germ because it has a deliciously nutty flavor and a pleasant crunchy texture. Sprinkle it over pasta instead of parmesan cheese or over a casserole instead of breadcrumbs. It can also be used to enhance the flavor and texture of baked goods, casseroles, and smoothies.

Whole-grain bread, flour, and pasta. Breads, flours, and pastas made with 100 percent whole grains have a superior nutritional profile to refined grains and also offer a complex, full-bodied texture and flavor. Look for the word "whole" on the package label. Sprouted whole-grain breads are a great choice, as the sprouting process enhances the nutritional value and digestibility of the bread. Sprouted breads are typically found in the freezer case. If you're looking for them in a conventional supermarket, check the section where other frozen natural foods are stocked.

Dried Herbs and Spices

Artful seasoning is the secret to creating flavorful fare without adding a lot of salt, sugar, or extra fat. Plus, herbs and spices often have admirable health benefits. I've incorporated a variety of these seasonings in the recipes in this book in keeping with how I cook day in, day out. I even use herbs and spices when cooking breakfast! Herbs and spices also give you an opportunity to tailor dishes to suit your tastes or please the palates of those you're cooking for. One of the easiest ways to jazz up any recipe and give it your own personal flair is to play with the seasonings.

The most common dried herbs and spices are readily available at most supermarkets. For more unusual varieties, look in the bulk herb section at natural food stores or spice shops. Purchasing in bulk is a good choice for herbs and spices you don't use often. This way you can buy just a small amount at a time to ensure maximum freshness and flavor. Store them in a cool, dark place away from sunlight or heat sources, such as the stovetop or oven.

Here's a basic list of the dried herbs and spices called for in this book. This is also a good, basic set of seasonings to keep on hand as the basis of your spice cabinet:

- basil
- cayenne
- chili powder
- cinnamon (ground)
- cumin (ground)
- crushed red pepper flakes
- dill weed
- fines herbes
- garlic powder
- italian seasoning
- paprika
- parsley
- pepper (freshly ground and coarse and fine preground black pepper)
- pumpkin pie spice
- rosemary
- sea salt (coarse and fine grind)
- turmeric

Fresh Herbs

Dried herbs are fine, but for incomparable flavor nothing beats fresh herbs, which add real pizzazz to salads, pastas, sandwiches, and soups. In most recipes you can substitute chopped, fresh herbs for dried. Because dried herbs are more concentrated than fresh, increase the amount; in general, use three times as much as the amount of dried herbs called for.

Although parsley, cilantro, and basil are typically available at markets in larger quantities, finding other herbs in good condition and at a reasonable price can be hit-or-miss. Fortunately, many herbs are hardy and easy to grow in the warmer months, and I heartily recommend you give it a try. You don't need much space. Even a window box or a few pots on your deck or a windowsill will suffice.

GROWING FRESH HERBS

If you are growing herbs outdoors, plant them as soon as possible after the threat of frost in your region has passed. Growing from seed takes much longer, so buy small plants, four to eight inches high, from a local nursery or farmers' market. Good choices include basil, cilantro, oregano, parsley, rosemary, and sage.

Transplant your starters into pots six to twelve inches in diameter, depending on the size of the plants you purchased. Make sure there are several drainage holes in the bottom of each pot. Fill the pot halfway to three-quarters full with potting soil. Carefully remove the herb plant from the pot it came in and position it in the middle of the larger pot. Add more potting soil around the plant to fill the pot. Pat the soil down firmly and water until the soil is moist but not oversaturated. Place the pot in a sunny area and water whenever the surface of the soil becomes dry to the touch. Pinch or cut off the herbs as needed.

STORING FRESH HERBS

It's best to use fresh herbs shortly after you harvest or purchase them. If you won't be using them right away, wrap them loosely in a paper towel and store them in a spacious container or plastic bag in the vegetable compartment of your refrigerator. Don't chop them until you're ready to use them. If you purchase a large bunch of herbs that still has the roots attached, you can store it in water, just like fresh flowers. First rinse the roots briefly, then place the herbs in a vase or glass of water and keep them on your kitchen counter. That way you can easily grab a few leaves as you cook. Although it's a bit unconventional, you can also use a vase of fresh herbs to decorate the dining table, especially at the end of summer when herbs such as basil start to bloom. This is a beautiful and beautifully scented eco-friendly centerpiece. If kept in a cool room out of direct sunlight, the herbs will keep for two to four days, depending upon the variety and freshness.

Keeping It Clean

You're probably interested in plant-based cookery for a number of reasons, but I'll bet that many of them boil down to one key concept: well-being—for yourself, for your family and friends, and for the environment that supports us all. I encourage you to keep this concept in mind not just when cooking, but also when cleaning your kitchen. These days there's no excuse not to, as there are so many nontoxic and environmentally friendly cleaning products available. I suggest that you experiment with different brands to find those that work best for you. When considering the many options, be sure to seek out products made with nontoxic, biodegradable ingredients and that are phosphate-free and (of course) not tested on animals. Recycled or at least recyclable packaging is always a plus.

My favorite all-purpose kitchen cleanser for daily light-duty cleaning is plain old baking soda. I put it in a shaker container that has fairly large holes on top. Then I use it to clean the sink, countertops, and oven. Just sprinkle some baking soda on the surface to be cleaned, scrub away the dirt and grime with a moist sponge or dish cloth, and then rinse or wipe with a clean, damp cloth.

Table of Equivalent Measures

Despite all the recipes I've developed, I never seem to completely memorize measurement equivalencies. In fact, I often find myself referring to the following table, especially when doubling or tripling recipes or dividing them to make smaller quantities. I hope you find this information handy too!

This . . .	Equals this . . .
3 teaspoons	1 tablespoon
4 tablespoons	¼ cup
8 tablespoons	½ cup
12 tablespoons	¾ cup
16 tablespoons	1 cup (or 8 fluid ounces)
2 cups	1 pint (or 16 fluid ounces)
4 cups	1 quart (or 32 fluid ounces)
4 quarts	1 gallon (or 128 fluid ounces)

Planning Tempting Menus

Whether you're serving a quick weekday breakfast or supper, hosting an elegant dinner party or holiday soiree, or offering brunch or a buffet, putting together an inviting and well-rounded menu will ensure optimum enjoyment of the meal. In this chapter I offer a few tips on menu planning in general and then provide twelve sample menus that demonstrate how to create a tempting and delicious bill of fare by selecting dishes that complement each other in taste, texture, and nutrition.

Basic Menu-Planning Tips

For evening meals on weeknights or busy weekends, look to one-pot dishes, such as casseroles, stews, chilis, or hearty soups. These are sure to satisfy hungry appetites yet often involve only minimal prep and cleanup time. To enhance or round-out a one-pot meal, serve crusty bread or a cooked whole grain on the side. A simple bowl of vegan ice cream makes the perfect dessert.

Lunch menus might focus on soup, salad, a sandwich, or a combination of these. For a hearty lunch on the go, a sandwich or wrap that incorporates baby greens, various veggies, and a bit of tofu or tempeh is a good choice. For more formal luncheon options, serve a light puréed soup as the first course and then feature a main dish salad or light entrée, such as stuffed artichokes, as the main course. For dessert, consider a fruit-based cake or fresh fruit salad.

Creating a spectacular dinner party menu can seem like a challenge. When entertaining, you may feel a lot of pressure for everything to go perfectly. This is natural. Even after twenty years of hosting vegan parties, both large and small, I still get anxious when figuring out my menu!

We all want to dazzle family and friends with tempting culinary creations. Just remember that another key to success is that everyone have an enjoyable evening—and that includes you. This is where a little advance planning goes a long way, allowing you to share your guests' pleasure in the meal and the evening.

If you're planning a meal with three or more courses, figure out your cooking timetable in advance. Consider serving a soup as the first course, and choose something you can make earlier in the day and then reheat before serving. A delicate salad is an elegant second course. To the extent possible, assemble the salad ingredients earlier in the day and then compose and dress the salad just before serving. A good choice for the entrée is a casserole or other baked dish that can be assembled in the morning, chilled, and then put in the oven to bake as you greet your guests and enjoy other courses. To finish the meal, serve a chilled or room-temperature dessert that you can make earlier in the day or even the previous day.

Jazzy Vegetarian Menu Plans

As promised, here are twelve delightful and delicious menus using recipes from this book. These menus are sufficiently varied that you're sure to find one to suit any occasion. To enhance your enjoyment, I've also suggested music to complement the meal, and it should come as no surprise that most are jazz selections. On my journey as a jazz musician and radio host, I've had the rare opportunity to meet many talented musicians, and I'm glad to have this opportunity to share some of my favorite recordings. Bon appétit!

MENU 1

Bountiful Brunch Buffet

This menu is an extravaganza. Don't fret; I'm not recommending that you prepare all of these for one meal. Rather, choose from the options listed below to fit the occasion, as well as your timeline and budget. For baked goods, I recommend oversized muffins or a trio of sweet, savory, and plain mini-biscuits. (For more muffin options, see chapter 4, and for other baked goods, see chapter 11.) For a main dish, choose among a scrambled tofu dish featuring mushrooms and red bell peppers, a delectable cashew-based French toast, or, for a simpler option, a quinoa porridge that will perk up the taste buds. For a simple side dish, I recommend a sliced tomato plate or a fruit salad, or offer both. Don't forget the fair-trade coffee and tea, nondairy milk, and organic juice!

BAKED GOODS

*Blueberry, Savory Herb, and
Plain Mini-Biscuits* (page 55)

Chocolate Chip–Banana Muffins (page 53)

MAIN DISHES

Cashew French Toast (page 38)

Cinnamon-Spiced Quinoa Porridge with Dried Fruit (page 32)

No-Egg Scramble (page 36)

SALADS

Fancy Fruit Salad (page 92)

Tomato-Basil Pinwheel (page 94)

JAZZY MUSIC PICK

Antonio Vivaldi, *The Four Seasons*

Okay, I admit it: this selection doesn't qualify as jazz. However, it is a familiar, elegant, and timeless piece of music—and the perfect choice to play as guests arrive and throughout the meal.

Summer Picnic

This delightful picnic menu is easy to make, breezy to serve, and ideal for dining alfresco. Plus, it's eco-friendly. Chilled soup served in edible bowls is paired with delectable avocado roll-ups—a salad in its own edible wrapping! Because no picnic would be complete without potato salad, this menu features my take on that classic. Portable peanut butter fudge rounds out the meal. Make sure to bring along plenty of cool drinks and springwater. Pack your everyday tableware or other reusable plates and utensils, and be sure to include a washable tablecloth, cloth napkins, and a cotton blanket.

SOUP

Cool Cucumber Soup (page 70),
served in bread bowls

MAIN DISHES

Avocado Rolls with Sunflower Seeds (page 88)
Country-Style Red Potato Salad (page 99)

DESSERT

Peanut Butter Fudge (page 182)

JAZZY MUSIC PICK

John Gatti, *Destinations*

This excellent album has a light and airy jazz feel and is perfectly attuned to a meal that's an outing, even if it's only in your own backyard. The songs are inspired by places that John and his wife have visited, from the Caribbean to the Jersey shore, and from Washington, DC, to Paris. Press the play button and escape to distant destinations.

MENU 3
Deli Delights

Crafting vegan versions of traditional deli dishes can be challenging, but this menu does just that. First up is a guilt-free pâté with all of the health benefits of walnuts, tofu, and green peas, followed by an eggless salad that offers a tasty twist on a time-honored deli staple. The star attraction is a vegan reuben sandwich paired with tasty oven fries. For dessert, an easy-to-make apple cake is sure to delight.

STARTER
Jazzy Vegetarian Not Liver (page 61)

SALAD
Eggless Egg Salad (page 102)

MAIN DISH
Reuben-Style Sandwiches (page 84)

SIDE DISH
Zesty Zucchini Oven Fries (page 163) *or*
Fabulous Oven Fries (page 162)

DESSERT
Upside-Down Apple Cake (page 188)

JAZZY MUSIC PICK

Laura Theodore and Don Rebic, *Tonight's the Night*

This was my debut release, and it continues to be one of my most popular recordings. It contains six originals that I cowrote with master pianist Don Rebic, and it was a *Musician Magazine* Best Unsigned Bands award winner. The idea for this recording sprouted one spring afternoon when my musical director and longtime friend Don Rebic called and said, "Let's write and produce our own jazz CD, featuring the type of music we enjoy playing." The result is tunes that are jazzy, optimistic, and lively, making a cheerful musical addition to any meal.

Farmers' Market Fresh Menu

This farm-fresh menu is inspired by late summer visits to my local farmers' market. It features easy recipes that are bursting with just-picked flavor. A refreshing gazpacho starts off the meal, offering a chilled delight on a hot summer day. For the salad, I've repurposed a recipe that appears in the side dish chapter: a savory raw mixture featuring zucchini "noodles." Since those aren't real noodles (and because I'm such a pasta enthusiast), the main dish is genuine pasta, tossed with a zippy arugula pesto. As fall draws near, apples become plentiful, so this menu concludes with a delicious apple crisp for dessert.

SOUP
Garden Vegetable Gazpacho (page 72)

SALAD
Zucchini Fettuccine with Fresh Tomato Salsa (page 148)

MAIN DISH
Arugula-and-Walnut Pesto Pasta (page 110)

DESSERT
Autumn Apple Crisp (page 192)

JAZZY MUSIC PICK

New York Voices, *New York Voices*

The debut album from this popular jazz vocal quintet is a mix of tightly woven, high-powered harmonies performed in a fresh pop-fusion style, including the favorites "Caravan" and "Round Midnight." The lineup of New York Voices has since changed, but this 1989 album remains among their best. The up-tempo, toe-tapping tunes make this recording a great backdrop to any farm-fresh menu.

MENU 5
Thirty-Minute Vegan

When you want a quick, healthful meal but are short on time, this menu is an ideal solution. It features a tangy pasta dish with fresh broccoli and sun-dried tomatoes, warm bakery bread, and a hearty salad. I've even included a refreshing banana-based frozen dessert. Best of all, everything can be ready in just thirty minutes.

SALAD

Avocado-Cashew Salad (page 96)

MAIN DISH

Quick Penne with Broccoli and Sun-Dried Tomatoes (page 108)

SIDE DISH

Warm Bakery Bread with Herbed Dipping Oil (page 170)

DESSERT

Frozen Banana Creamy with Cocoa Dust (page 176)

JAZZY MUSIC PICK

Third World Love, *New Blues*

With its lyrical and emotional feel, this album is the perfect way to wind down and change your mood on a busy weeknight evening. Third World Love is four international up-and-coming young jazz musicians who shine on this exciting recording of mostly original music. The recommended selection to begin the meal is the beautiful "Joy of Life," which features talented trumpeter Avishai Cohen and rock-steady drummer Daniel Freedman.

Meatless Meatloaf Supper

This menu is based on a wonderful vegan rendition of traditional meatloaf and mashed potatoes, updated to be more nutritious and waistline-friendly without sacrificing beloved flavors and textures. The meatless loaf features mushrooms and omega-3-rich walnuts, the mashed potatoes are lightened up and given a nutritional boost with cauliflower, and the green beans are dressed up with sesame seeds. With a classic chocolate cake for dessert to round out the meal, this is a menu you'll be confident to serve to anyone.

MAIN DISH

Wonderful Walnut-Mushroom Loaf (page 130)

SIDE DISHES

Mashed Potatoes and Cauliflower (page 158)

Sesame Green Beans (page 150)

DESSERT

Double-Chocolate Cake (page 185)

JAZZY MUSIC PICK

Terry Blaine, *With Thee I Swing*

Ms. Blaine's upbeat, vibrant, and cheerful vocal style will enhance any gathering. *With Thee I Swing* features Terry at her best as she masterfully weaves her way through familiar selections such as "What a Little Moonlight Can Do" and "I Got Rhythm." This live album is sure to lend an upbeat mood to the meal, and Terry's interpretation of traditional classics will perfectly complement this jazzy take on traditional fare.

Italian Flair

In this Italian-inspired meal, easy-to-make lasagna rolls stand front and center. They're backed up by a harmonious trio of roasted bell peppers, broccoli rabe, and ever-popular garlic bread. A refreshing dish of strawberries lightly bathed in a balsamic syrup provides the perfect coda to finish the meal.

MAIN DISH

Quick Lasagna Rolls (page 120)

SIDE DISHES

Basil Roasted Peppers (page 160)

Grandma's Garlic Bread (page 171)

Nino's Broccoli Rabe with Garlic (page 153)

DESSERT

Balsamic Strawberry Delight (page 174)

JAZZY MUSIC PICK

Micheal Castaldo, *Aceto*

Aceto, singer-songwriter Micheal Castaldo's third album, honors his late father, Pasquale. It includes fourteen classic and two original Italian songs that evoke feelings of grace, healing, and remembrance. Melodic and passionate, it resonates with the full-flavored dishes in this menu. By the way, *aceto* means "vinegar" in Italian, so you must play that particular cut when serving the delicate, vinegar-laced strawberries for dessert!

Southwestern Menu

This menu features easy Southwestern-style recipes that are bursting with festive flavor. It starts with a velvety guacamole dip that can be whipped up in a flash and a healthier twist on nachos—fun fare that you can prepare in only fifteen minutes, and that kids will love. Chili with hearty homemade cornbread is a natural pairing. To top it all off, what could be better than a rich and satisfying chocolate pudding with just a hint of spicy heat?

STARTERS

Five-Ingredient Guacamole Dip (page 60)

Nutritious Nachos (page 64)

MAIN DISH

Jazzy Black Bean Chili (page 135)

SIDE DISH

Double-Corn Cornbread (page 57)

DESSERT

Sweet-and-Spicy Chocolate Mousse (page 175)

JAZZY MUSIC PICK

Maria Postell, *At This Moment*

Vocalist Maria Postell's release *At This Moment* will transport you to an intimate jazz club from an earlier era. Her vibrant vocals on such standards as "My Foolish Heart" and "At Last" will add a spicy note to your auditory environment to accentuate the piquant fare in this menu.

Festive Lasagna Dinner

Whether you're feeding family or friends, lasagna is always guaranteed to please, and it plays the starring role in this more formal menu. The opening attraction is a light and lovely soup, and the second course is a simple yet elegant salad. Fresh berries with a sweet and creamy topping finish the meal with a flourish.

SOUP

Carrot and Orzo Soup (page 76)

SALAD

Mixed Baby Greens Salad (page 95)

MAIN DISH

Festive Zucchini Lasagna (page 116)

DESSERT

Raspberry-Maple Tofu Whip (page 193)
with fresh berries

JAZZY MUSIC PICK

Michael Feinstein, *Fly Me to the Moon*

This elegant and melodious recording has the perfect mix of pop-jazz selections to enhance this menu. Mr. Feinstein is an impeccable performer and vocalist, a musical archivist, and a vegan! *Fly Me to the Moon* features him at his best, accompanied by guitar great Joe Negri.

MENU 10
Party Portobello Dinner

Whatever the occasion may be, if you're hosting a soiree, this uncomplicated merrymaking menu is sure to please. It begins with an elegant yet earthy composed salad, awakening taste buds for the main event: portobello mushrooms encrusted in a savory crunchy coating. On the side, delicate spears of roasted asparagus and a cloud of mashed sweet potatoes hit just the right notes to complement the meaty, mouthwatering mushrooms. Fruity parfaits end the meal on a light and delicate sweet note. If you're looking for a meal that's guaranteed to impress, this is the menu to try.

SALAD

Walnut, Beet, and Tofu Salad (page 101)

MAIN DISH

Crispy Portobello Steaks (page 128)

SIDE DISHES

Maple Sweet Potatoes (page 163)
Roasted Asparagus with Garlic and Tomatoes (page 165)

DESSERT

Luscious Raspberry Parfaits (page 177)

JAZZY MUSIC PICK

Joe Beck, *Finger Painting*

Many people consider Joe Beck to have been the finest guitarist in jazz history. He was the first guitar player to work with Miles Davis and also accompanied such greats as Frank Sinatra, Paul Simon, James Brown, and Peggy Lee. The music in this collection is upbeat yet relaxing—and totally top-notch—making it the perfect complement to this menu.

MENU 11

Company Is Coming

This tried-and-true formal menu is one of my favorite meals to serve when guests are coming for dinner. The first course, a rich and creamy carrot soup, is followed by my go-to salad of baby greens tossed with a simple balsamic vinaigrette. Then it's time for the showstopping entrée: colorful stuffed bell peppers, with a dressed-up kale dish on the side. A super-simple yet spectacular pudding ends the meal on a high note.

SOUP

Velvety Carrot Soup (page 78)

SALAD

Mixed Baby Greens Salad (page 95)

MAIN DISH

Fancy Stuffed Peppers with Quinoa and Black Beans (page 142)

SIDE DISH

Sweet-and-Savory Kale (page 151)

DESSERT

Chocolate Ganache Pudding (page 179)

JAZZY MUSIC PICK

Jim Brickman, *Home*

Mr. Brickman, touted as America's romantic piano sensation, really shines on this soothing recording, which echoes the welcome feeling of being with family and friends. *Home* is a mix of beautiful solo piano pieces and upbeat vocal selections, such as "Thank You," featuring the soulful voice of Matt Giraud. This recording is guaranteed to keep the energy flowing during an evening get-together.

Happy Holiday Menu

oliday meals can be difficult for vegetarians. Family and friends may feel uncertain what to cook for you, and you may feel the same way in regard to them. The answer is this menu, which will please all diners at any holiday dinner party or festive family meal. A sweet potato soup starts the meal with familiar and comforting flavors, allowing you to slip in a salad that's on the unusual side, featuring figs and kale. Everyone will savor the main course: either portobello mushrooms or acorn squash, both featuring a scrumptious savory stuffing. A variety of side dishes are listed for you to mix and match as you desire. A delectable, homemade spice cake redolent with fruits and nuts is the perfect way to finish this menu on a traditional note.

SOUP

Savory Sweet Potato Soup (page 81)

SALAD

Fig, Kale, and Tomato Salad (page 98)

MAIN DISH

Perfect Party Portobellos (page 144) *or*
Stuffed Acorn Squash (page 137)

SIDE DISHES

Mashed Potatoes and Cauliflower (page 158)

Sweet-and-Savory Kale (page 151) *or*
Sesame Green Beans (page 150)

Yam Casserole (page 164) *or*
Maple Sweet Potatoes (page 163)

DESSERT

Fruit and Nut Spice Cake (page 184)

JAZZY MUSIC PICK

Joe Beck and Laura Theodore, *Golden Earrings*

I guess I'll take this opportunity to toot my own horn. This album, as described by *Jazz Review*, is "a memorable duo recording that is destined to become a classic of its kind with its impeccable, perfect performances by Beck and Theodore. Joe Beck was always a fine guitarist, and in this collection, he shines. His performances are subtle and complex. . . . . Laura Theodore remains one of the finest jazz singers in contemporary jazz, and her voice is at its finest in these well-crafted performances. . . . Highly recommended." I hope you'll enjoy playing this recording at your next merrymaking holiday celebration!

Jazzy Tip If you're new to vegan eating, start by serving a nonmeat meal a few times a week for dinner, preparing hearty favorites like veggie chili, vegetarian lasagna, or spaghetti with marinara sauce.

Bountiful Breakfasts and Smoothies

Fancy Fruit Salad, 92, and No-Egg Scramble, 36

Breakfast does just that, *breaks* our overnight *fast*. If you think of it that way, it's obvious why breakfast is often said to be the *most important meal of the day.* Some of us like a quick, light option, and others crave a large, filling meal. Either way, incorporating fresh and nutritious ingredients into your first meal of the day will get you started off on the right foot. Smoothies make a great choice for breakfast on the go, while scrambled tofu or vegan french toast is a hearty option to satisfy a big appetite. Whatever your breakfast style, you'll find some tasty recipes in this chapter. *Good morning!*

Quinoa is often thought of as just a supper staple, but it makes a wonderful breakfast food too. It is rich in fiber and high-quality protein, and its great taste is sure to jump-start your day.

Cinnamon-Spiced Quinoa Porridge with Dried Fruit

MAKES 3 TO 4 SERVINGS

2 cups water

1 cup quinoa, rinsed thoroughly

2 tablespoons raisins

1 tablespoon dried cranberries or cherries

1 teaspoon vegan margarine

½ teaspoon ground cinnamon

1 tablespoon brown sugar or maple syrup (optional), plus more for serving

Nondairy milk, for serving

Put the water, quinoa, raisins, cranberries, margarine, and cinnamon in a medium saucepan and bring to a boil over medium heat. Decrease the heat to low, cover, and cook for about 15 minutes, until the water is absorbed and the quinoa is soft but not mushy.

Remove from the heat and give the quinoa a stir to fluff it up. Sprinkle the optional brown sugar evenly over the top. Cover and let sit until the sugar melts, 3 to 5 minutes. Spoon into cereal bowls. Serve hot, with nondairy milk and more brown sugar if desired.

When I was a child, my mom sometimes served white rice left over from dinner as breakfast fare. She would add milk, heat it up, and serve it with sugar, just like porridge. It was always a favorite of mine. This recipe uses brown rice, rather than white, making it more wholesome, and the dried fruit adds plenty of natural sugar, so no extra sweetener is needed.

Breakfast Rice with Sweet Spices

2¼ cups water

1 cup long-grain brown rice, rinsed

1 to 2 tablespoons raisins

1 to 2 tablespoons dried cranberries or cherries

¼ teaspoon sea salt

¼ teaspoon ground cinnamon

¼ teaspoon pumpkin pie spice (optional)

Nondairy milk, for serving

Put the water, rice, raisins, cranberries, salt, cinnamon, and optional pumpkin pie spice in a medium saucepan and bring to a boil over medium-high heat. Decrease the heat to medium-low, cover, and cook for 35 to 40 minutes, until the water is absorbed and the rice is very tender.

Remove from the heat and give the rice a stir to fluff it up. Cover and let sit for 5 to 10 minutes to finish cooking. Spoon into cereal bowls. Serve hot, with nondairy milk if desired.

The tender texture of cooked barley pairs beautifully with raisins in this sweet breakfast porridge. It tastes great on its own, but a splash of nondairy milk and a drizzle of maple syrup will add layers of flavor to this unique morning treat.

Breakfast Barley

MAKES 4 SERVINGS

4 cups water

1 cup pearl barley

⅓ cup raisins

Maple syrup, for serving

Nondairy milk, for serving

Put the water, barley, and raisins in a medium saucepan and bring to a boil over medium-high heat. Decrease the heat to medium-low, cover, and cook for 45 to 60 minutes, until the barley is tender and the water is absorbed. Serve hot, topped with nondairy milk and maple syrup if desired.

This quick and creamy staple has been kid and husband tested and approved. It packs a lot of nutrition in the most flavor-filled bowl of oatmeal ever, and it just might reignite your family's joy in breakfast.

Awesome Oatmeal

4 cups water

2 cups old-fashioned rolled oats

3 tablespoons raisins or dried cranberries, or a combination

2 tablespoons toasted sunflower seeds (optional)

⅛ teaspoon sea salt

1 to 2 tablespoons brown sugar or maple syrup

Nondairy milk (optional)

Put the water, oats, raisins, optional sunflower seeds, and salt in a large saucepan. Bring to a boil over medium heat. Decrease the heat to medium-low and cook, stirring occasionally, until most of the liquid has been absorbed and the mixture is creamy. Remove from the heat and sweeten with the brown sugar to taste. Cover and let sit for about 5 minutes before serving. Serve with nondairy milk and more sweetener if desired.

NOTE: After the oatmeal is cooked, it will stay warm for about 20 minutes in the covered saucepan, which is ideal for family members who trickle in for breakfast.

If you've been missing scrambled eggs, then this is the dish for you. For a hearty breakfast, serve the scramble with whole-grain toast, vegan bacon or sausage, and fruit on the side. When I serve this dish family-style, I spoon the hot scramble into a covered serving tureen so it stays warm at the table.

No-Egg Scramble

MAKES 2 TO 3 SERVINGS

1 tablespoon extra-virgin olive oil, plus more as needed

1 onion, chopped

5 ounces cremini or white button mushrooms, sliced

½ bell pepper, any color, chopped

½ to 1 teaspoon reduced-sodium tamari

14 to 16 ounces firm regular tofu, drained

½ teaspoon ground turmeric

⅛ teaspoon cayenne

⅛ teaspoon sea salt

½ cup grated vegan cheese (optional)

Freshly ground pepper

Heat the oil in a large skillet over medium heat. Add the onion and cook, stirring occasionally, until slightly softened, about 5 minutes. Add the mushrooms and cook, stirring occasionally, for 1 minute. Add the peppers and ½ teaspoon of the tamari and cook, stirring occasionally, until the onion is slightly golden, about 20 minutes.

Meanwhile, put the tofu in a medium bowl and mash with a potato masher or large fork until crumbly. Add the turmeric, cayenne, salt, and ¼ teaspoon of the tamari. Mash until the tofu resembles the color and texture of cooked scrambled eggs.

Add the tofu to the skillet, adding more oil and a bit more tamari if the mixture seems dry. Cook, stirring frequently, until the scramble is heated through and the tofu is lightly browned

on the edges. Scatter the optional vegan cheese over the top and season with pepper to taste. Cover the skillet tightly, remove from the heat, and let the vegan cheese melt for 4 to 5 minutes. Serve immediately.

Jazzy Tip Turmeric, a member of the ginger family, is a great spice to add to your vegan recipe repertoire. Its stunning yellow-orange color enhances the visual appeal of many dishes, and its mild but unmistakable flavor imparts depth. It is touted as having numerous health benefits and has long been used in both Chinese and Ayurvedic medicine. Try adding turmeric to classic rice and beans, a tofu and veggie sauté, or a wide variety of recipes made with tofu, tempeh, grains, or vegetables.

After numerous failed attempts at making vegan french toast, I was determined to develop a foolproof version. I discovered that cashews make a rich, thick mixture, perfect for dipping the bread into. Voilà! Vegan french toast that rivals the best of conventional recipes. Serve it warm, liberally drizzled with maple syrup.

Cashew French Toast

MAKES 3 TO 4 SERVINGS

1 cup raw cashews

1 cup water

¼ teaspoon ground cinnamon

¼ teaspoon vanilla extract

5 to 6 slices sprouted whole-grain bread

Maple syrup, for serving

Put the cashews, water, cinnamon, and vanilla extract in a blender and process until smooth. Pour the mixture into a shallow bowl or pie pan. Dip both sides of each slice of bread into the cashew mixture until thoroughly coated, then place them in a single layer on a large, rimmed baking sheet. Use a fork to poke several holes in each slice. Spoon any remaining cashew mixture over the bread. Refrigerate for 30 to 60 minutes to allow the bread to completely absorb the cashew mixture.

Put a thin layer of vegetable oil in a large skillet over medium heat. When it is hot but not smoking, put several slices

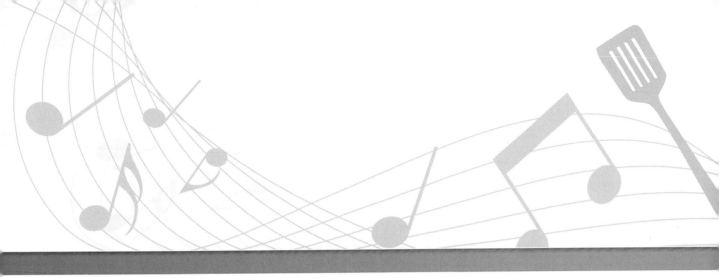

of the bread in the skillet, cover, and cook until the underside is golden brown and crispy, 3 to 5 minutes. Flip each slice and cook until the other side is golden brown and crispy, adding more oil as needed to prevent sticking. Transfer to a serving plate. Cook the remaining slices the same way. Serve hot, with maple syrup on the side for drizzling.

NOTE: To keep the first batch of french toast warm while the remainder is cooking, transfer it to a baking sheet and put it in an oven preheated to 300 degrees F.

This smoothie is truly delightful, especially when strawberries are in season.

Strawberry Delight Smoothie

2 cups fresh or frozen strawberries

2 frozen bananas (see note)

2 cups sweetened plain or vanilla nondairy milk

3 tablespoons raw or toasted wheat germ

Put all the ingredients in a blender and process until smooth. Serve immediately.

NOTE: To freeze bananas, break each one into 3 or 4 pieces and put them in a ziplock freezer bag. Seal and freeze for at least 12 hours before using.

With its tart and tangy flavors, this smoothie is a rejuvenating early morning or midafternoon pick-me-up.

Refreshing Citrus Smoothie

5 stalks celery, with leaves, cut into 2-inch slices

1 apple, cored and quartered

1 orange, peeled and quartered

1 teaspoon freshly squeezed lemon juice

½ to 1 cup filtered water

Put the celery, apple, orange, lemon juice, and ½ cup of the water in a blender. Process until smooth, adding more water as needed to achieve the desired consistency. Serve immediately.

Thanks to wheat germ and almonds, this satisfying shake offers a good protein boost. Although soaking the almonds requires advance planning, it's worth it for the extra-creamy texture the soaked nuts impart.

Banana-Almond Super Shake

8 to 10 raw almonds, soaked in filtered water to cover for 8 to 12 hours and drained

2 fresh or frozen bananas (see note, page 40)

1 cup plain or vanilla nondairy milk

5 or 6 ice cubes (optional)

1 tablespoon raw or toasted wheat germ

1½ teaspoons flaxseed meal or freshly ground flaxseeds (optional)

½ to 1 cup filtered water

Put the almonds in a colander and rinse under cool water. Drain. Transfer to a blender and add the bananas, nondairy milk, optional ice cubes, wheat germ, optional flaxseed meal, and ½ cup of the water. Process until smooth and creamy, adding more water as needed to achieve the desired consistency. Serve immediately.

An unusual combination of fresh fruits and vegetables gives this smoothie its pretty pink hue.

Sunrise Smoothie

MAKES 2 TO 3 SERVINGS

1 apple, cored and quartered

1 pear, cored and quartered

3 stalks celery, with leaves, cut into 2-inch pieces

1 carrot, peeled and cut into 2-inch pieces

1 cup filtered water

½ cup frozen blueberries

4 or 5 ice cubes

2 to 3 teaspoons freshly squeezed lemon juice

Put all the ingredients in a blender and process until smooth. Serve immediately.

Jazzy Tip Have you just squeezed a lemon? Don't throw it away yet! To clean and freshen up your sink, just turn the lemon rind inside out and use it to scrub your sink, then rinse thoroughly with fresh water. Try this with a lime or grapefruit too!

Start your day in a happy way with this fun and delicious green-tinged smoothie. The ice cubes are optional but recommended for the frostiness factor.

Happy Start Smoothie

2 large carrots, peeled and cut into 2-inch pieces

2 apples, cored and quartered

3 to 4 large leaves romaine lettuce

1 cup filtered water

½ cup chopped fresh parsley

6 ice cubes (optional)

Put all the ingredients in a blender and process until smooth. Serve immediately.

I often start my day with this enticing and energizing combination of berries, bananas, and baby greens. Using frozen bananas makes for an extra-thick smoothie.

Raspberry-Banana Green Dream Smoothie

MAKES 2 SERVINGS

2 fresh or frozen bananas (see note, page 40)

1½ ounces (2 cups, lightly packed) **mixed baby greens**

1 to 1½ cups frozen raspberries or blueberries

1 to 2 cups filtered water

Put the bananas, greens, berries, and 1 cup of the water in a blender. Process until smooth, adding more water as needed to achieve the desired consistency. Serve immediately.

Jazzy Tip Always keep bags of frozen raspberries, blueberries, and strawberries in your freezer. These sweet, convenient fruits will help you to make breakfast smoothies and creamy desserts in a flash.

This tropical-inspired smoothie adds a bit of green to your day in a delightful way. The banana provides a sweet taste and creamy texture, while the pineapple adds a bit of tang.

Tropical Green Smoothie

MAKES 2 TO 3 SERVINGS

1½ **ounces** (2 cups, lightly packed) **mixed baby greens or baby spinach**

2 cups coarsely chopped pineapple

2 fresh or frozen bananas
(see note, page 40)

4 ice cubes (optional)

1½ **to 2 cups filtered water**

Put the greens, pineapple, bananas, optional ice cubes, and ¾ cup of the water in a blender. Process until smooth and creamy, adding more water as needed to achieve the desired consistency. Serve immediately.

Scrumptious Muffins and Quick Breads

Luscious Little Carrot Muffins, 50

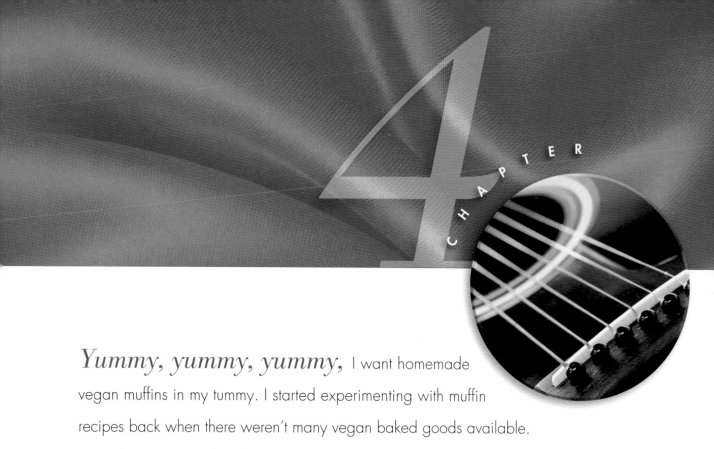

Yummy, yummy, yummy, I want homemade vegan muffins in my tummy. I started experimenting with muffin recipes back when there weren't many vegan baked goods available. Over the years I've developed some foolproof and easy techniques and a wide variety of recipes. In this chapter I share some of my favorites. All are enhanced with healthful ingredients like fruits, vegetables, or nuts, and some are on *the decadent side,* with a generous dose of chocolate chips. I'm willing to bet that once you get the hang of this basic method, *you'll never go back to store-bought muffins and quick breads.*

With their combination of fruit, nuts, summer squash, and homemade oat flour, these muffins make a bountiful breakfast or satisfying snack. The zucchini provides moisture, the nuts contribute crunch, and the fruit adds a beautiful color and fresh taste. This is an ideal recipe to bake during the summer months when zucchini is plentiful.

Apple, Raspberry, and Zucchini Muffins

MAKES 6 LARGE MUFFINS

1 cup rolled oats

1 cup whole wheat pastry flour

½ cup whole wheat flour

1 tablespoon baking powder

¼ teaspoon ground cinnamon

¼ teaspoon sea salt

⅓ cup brown sugar

1 apple, peeled, cored, and diced

½ zucchini, shredded

1 cup walnuts, chopped

1 cup plain or vanilla nondairy milk, plus more as needed

½ cup vegan margarine, melted

6 ounces raspberries

Preheat the oven to 400 degrees F. Oil a six-cup standard muffin tin.

Put the oats in a blender and process into a coarse flour. Transfer to a large bowl. Add the pastry flour, whole wheat flour, baking powder, cinnamon, and salt and stir with a dry whisk to combine. Add the brown sugar and stir with the whisk to combine. Add the apple, zucchini, and walnuts and stir until coated with the flour. Stir in the nondairy milk and margarine and mix just until incorporated. Gently fold in the raspberries. The mixture will be quite thick, but if it seems overly dry, stir in a bit more nondairy milk, 1 tablespoon at a time. Don't overmix or the muffins will be tough.

Mound the mixture into the prepared muffin cups. Put the pan on a baking sheet and bake for 20 minutes. Decrease the temperature to 375 degrees F and bake for 20 to 25 minutes, until golden and a toothpick inserted in the center of a muffin comes out clean.

Put the pan on a wire rack and loosen the sides of each muffin with a knife. Let cool for about 15 minutes. Carefully remove the muffins. Serve warm or at room temperature.

Jazzy Tip Toasting brings out the exquisite flavor of nuts and seeds, and it's very easy to do. Toasted nuts and seeds can replace raw ones in baked goods or other recipes. To toast nuts or seeds, preheat the oven to 325 degrees F. Spread the nuts or seeds in a single layer on a baking sheet or in a baking pan. Bake for 5 to 10 minutes, stirring or shaking the pan once or twice, until the nuts or seeds are evenly toasted and fragrant. Transfer to a plate to cool.

These muffins feature almond butter, which does double duty and stands in for both eggs and oil. The surprise comes when you bite into a muffin and discover a burst of beautiful blueberry preserves in the middle. In addition to being great for breakfast, these make a great snack or dessert. Feel free to improvise and use different types of preserves; raspberry and cherry are especially nice.

Blueberry Surprise Muffins

⅓ cup maple syrup

3 heaping tablespoons almond butter

2 cups whole wheat flour

2 teaspoons baking powder

½ teaspoon baking soda

¼ teaspoon sea salt

⅓ cup dried cranberries, sweetened or unsweetened

⅓ cup raisins

1½ cups plain or vanilla nondairy milk

¼ cup blueberry preserves or jam

Preheat the oven to 400 degrees F. Oil a six-cup standard muffin tin.

Put the maple syrup and almond butter in a small bowl and stir vigorously until well combined. Put the flour, baking powder, baking soda, and salt in a large bowl and stir with a dry whisk to combine. Stir in the cranberries and raisins. Stir in the nondairy milk and maple syrup mixture to make a batter. Mix just until incorporated. The batter will be quite thick. Don't overmix or the muffins will be tough.

Fill each prepared muffin cup one-third full with the batter. Make a small well in the center with a spoon or your finger. Spoon 2 teaspoons of the preserves into the well. Top with the remaining batter, distributing it evenly among the muffin cups.

Bake for 20 minutes. Decrease the temperature to 375 degrees F and bake for 20 to 25 minutes, until golden and a toothpick inserted in the center of a muffin comes out clean.

Put the pan on a wire rack and loosen the sides of each muffin with a knife. Let cool for about 15 minutes. Carefully remove the muffins. Serve warm or at room temperature.

These mini-muffins are on the larger side and perfect for an impressive breakfast, brunch, or even dessert. Although the frosting and garnish are optional, they create a stunning presentation.

Luscious Little Carrot Muffins

VEGAN CREAM CHEESE FROSTING (optional)

12 ounces vegan cream cheese, at room temperature

¾ cup confectioners' sugar, plus more as needed

1 teaspoon vanilla extract

CARROT GARNISH (optional)

⅓ cup peeled and grated carrot

MUFFINS

2½ cups whole wheat pastry flour

1 teaspoon baking powder

1 teaspoon baking soda

1 teaspoon ground cinnamon

½ teaspoon sea salt

½ cup brown sugar

1 cup finely chopped walnuts

1 cup peeled and grated carrots

¾ cup raisins

1 cup plain or vanilla nondairy milk

½ cup vegetable oil

½ cup maple syrup

1 teaspoon vanilla extract

Preheat the oven to 375 degrees F. Line two twelve-cup mini-muffin tins with paper liners.

To make the frosting, put the vegan cream cheese, confectioners' sugar, and vanilla extract in a medium bowl and stir vigorously until smooth and well blended. Cover and refrigerate for 1 to 24 hours.

Put the optional carrot garnish in a small bowl. Cover and refrigerate.

To make the muffins, put the flour, baking powder, baking soda, cinnamon, and salt in a large bowl and stir with a dry whisk to combine. Add the brown sugar and stir with the whisk to combine. Add the walnuts, carrots, and raisins and stir until coated with the flour. Stir in the nondairy milk, oil, maple syrup, and vanilla extract and mix just until incorporated.

Divide the mixture among the lined muffin cups. The muffin cups will be very full. Bake for 20 to 25 minutes, until golden and a toothpick inserted in the center of a muffin comes out clean.

Put the pans on wire racks and loosen the sides of each muffin with a knife. Let cool for about 15 minutes. Carefully remove the muffins from the pans (you may need to cut the tops apart before

removing them from the pans if they have over-flowed and fused together). Let cool for about 40 minutes longer.

Spoon a generous amount of frosting over the top of each muffin. Top with a bit of the carrot garnish, placed artfully in the center of the frosting. Covered tightly and stored in the refrigerator, leftover mini-muffins will keep for about 2 days.

NOTE: Use the frosting from this recipe to top a wide variety of cakes and other baked treats.

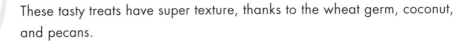

These tasty treats have super texture, thanks to the wheat germ, coconut, and pecans.

Coconut-Banana Muffins

2 cups whole wheat flour

1 tablespoon baking powder

1 teaspoon ground cinnamon

¼ teaspoon sea salt

1 cup raw or toasted unsweetened shredded dried coconut

1 cup chopped pecans or walnuts

½ cup toasted wheat germ

1¼ cups plain or vanilla nondairy milk, plus more as needed

2 ripe bananas, mashed until smooth

½ cup maple syrup

⅓ cup coconut oil, melted, or vegetable oil

Preheat the oven to 400 degrees F. Oil a six-cup standard muffin tin.

Put the flour, baking powder, cinnamon, and salt in a large bowl and stir with a dry whisk to combine. Add the coconut, pecans, and wheat germ and stir with the whisk to combine. Stir in the nondairy milk, bananas, maple syrup, and coconut oil and mix just until incorporated. The mixture will be quite thick, but if it seems overly dry, stir in a bit more nondairy milk, 1 tablespoon at a time. Don't overmix or the muffins will be tough.

Mound the mixture into the prepared muffin cups. Put the pan on a baking sheet and bake for 20 minutes. Decrease the temperature to 375 degrees F and bake for 20 to 25 minutes, until golden and a toothpick inserted in the middle of a muffin comes out clean.

Put the pan on a wire rack and loosen the sides of each muffin with a knife. Let cool for about 15 minutes. Carefully remove the muffins. Serve warm or at room temperature.

Jazzy Tip Try using mashed bananas or blended tofu to replace eggs in many baked goods recipes—about ¼ cup per egg is usually sufficient. This works especially well for most muffins, brownies, or basic cakes.

These moist muffins are sweet but not overly so, making them a scrumptious treat for breakfast, an afternoon snack, or dessert. This recipe uses ripe bananas rather than eggs for binding. Wheat germ adds both texture and nutrition, while dark chocolate contributes antioxidants, not to mention a decadent taste.

Chocolate Chip–Banana Muffins

see photo, page iv

MAKES 6 LARGE MUFFINS

1 cup whole wheat flour

1 cup whole wheat pastry flour

1 tablespoon baking powder

½ teaspoon sea salt

½ cup brown sugar

½ cup toasted wheat germ

1¼ cups plain or vanilla nondairy milk, plus more as needed

3 ripe bananas, mashed until smooth

¼ cup vegetable oil

½ cup vegan dark chocolate chips

3½ ounces vegan dark chocolate, chopped

Preheat the oven to 400 degrees F. Oil a six-cup standard muffin tin.

Put the flours, baking powder, and salt in a large bowl and stir with a dry whisk to combine. Add the brown sugar and wheat germ and stir with the whisk to combine. Stir in the nondairy milk, bananas, and oil and mix just until incorporated. Stir in the chocolate chips and chopped chocolate. The mixture will be quite thick, but if it seems overly dry, stir in a bit more nondairy milk, 1 tablespoon at a time. Don't overmix or the muffins will be tough.

Mound the mixture into the prepared muffin cups. Put the pan on a baking sheet and bake for 20 minutes. Decrease the temperature to 375 degrees F and bake for 20 to 25 minutes, until golden and a toothpick inserted in the middle of a muffin comes out clean.

Put the pan on a wire rack and loosen the sides of each muffin with a knife. Let cool for about 15 minutes. Carefully remove the muffins. Serve warm or at room temperature.

These semisweet muffins make a satisfying after-school snack or midafternoon pick-me-up and are also great as an on-the-go breakfast. The banana and apples provide sweetness, so only a bit of added sweetener is required, while the cocoa adds a hint of rich flavor.

Apple, Oat, and Cocoa Muffins

MAKES 6 LARGE MUFFINS

2 cups whole wheat flour

½ cup rolled oats

2 tablespoons unsweetened cocoa powder

1 tablespoon baking powder

½ teaspoon ground cinnamon

¼ teaspoon sea salt

3 apples, peeled, cored, and diced

1 cup plain or vanilla nondairy milk, plus more as needed

1 ripe banana, mashed until smooth

⅓ cup vegetable oil

¼ cup maple syrup

Preheat the oven to 400 degrees F. Oil a six-cup standard muffin tin.

Put the flour, oats, cocoa powder, baking powder, cinnamon, and salt in a large bowl and stir with a dry whisk to combine. Add the apples and stir until coated with the flour. Stir in the nondairy milk, banana, oil, and maple syrup and mix just until incorporated. The mixture will be quite thick, but if it seems overly dry, stir in a bit more nondairy milk, 1 tablespoon at a time. Don't overmix or the muffins will be tough.

Mound the mixture into the prepared muffin cups. Put the pan on a baking sheet and bake for 20 minutes. Decrease the temperature to 375 degrees F and bake for 20 to 25 minutes, until golden and a toothpick inserted in the center of a muffin comes out clean.

Put the pan on a wire rack and loosen the sides of each muffin with a knife. Let cool for about 15 minutes. Carefully remove the muffins. Serve warm or at room temperature.

A friend once told me that I should sell these biscuits so everyone could have a chance to taste them. Better yet, I'm providing the recipe so you can make them at home. They're easy to put together, even if you've never made biscuits before. Crunchy on the outside and tender on the inside, they have a delicate flavor that makes a pleasing addition not just to breakfast and brunch, but also to lunch or an evening meal. They're an ideal accompaniment for No-Egg Scramble (page 36).

Blueberry Mini-Biscuits

1 cup whole wheat flour

1 cup whole wheat pastry flour

1 tablespoon baking powder

¼ to ½ teaspoon sea salt

2 tablespoons toasted wheat germ

2 teaspoons brown sugar

1¼ cups unsweetened nondairy milk

⅓ cup vegan mayonnaise

½ teaspoon vanilla extract

1½ cups fresh blueberries

Preheat the oven to 400 degrees F. Oil two twelve-cup mini-muffin tins.

Put the flours, baking powder, and salt in a large bowl and stir with a dry whisk to combine. Add the wheat germ and brown sugar and stir with the whisk to combine.

Put the nondairy milk, vegan mayonnaise, and vanilla extract in a small bowl and whisk briskly until smooth and well combined. Pour into the flour mixture and stir just until incorporated and lump-free. The mixture will be quite thick. Gently fold in the blueberries.

Divide the mixture evenly among the prepared muffin cups. Bake for 18 to 22 minutes, until the tops are slightly golden.

Put the pan on a wire rack and loosen the sides of each biscuit with a knife. Let cool for about 15 minutes. Carefully remove the biscuits. Serve warm or at room temperature.

PLAIN MINI-BISCUITS: Omit the vanilla extract and blueberries and proceed as directed. Plain Mini-Biscuits are the perfect pairing with Jazzy Black Bean Chili (page 135) or Warming Winter Soup (page 82).

SAVORY HERB MINI-BISCUITS: Omit the vanilla extract and blueberries and add 4 to 5 leaves of fresh sage, minced, and 8 to 9 leaves of fresh basil, minced. Savory Herb Mini-Biscuits pair well with Cool Cucumber Soup (page 70), Velvety Carrot Soup (page 78), or any green salad.

This bread can be whipped together early in the morning or prepared the night before. The fruit, nuts, and wheat germ give it a well-rounded nutritional profile, making it a wholesome meal in a slice.

Bountiful Breakfast Bread

MAKES 6 TO 8 SERVINGS

2 cups whole wheat flour

⅓ cup toasted wheat germ

1 tablespoon baking powder

1 teaspoon pumpkin pie spice
or ground cinnamon

¼ teaspoon sea salt

2 small apples, peeled, cored, and chopped

½ cup raisins

½ cup dried cranberries

½ cup chopped pecans

⅓ cup unsalted roasted sunflower seeds

1¼ cups plain or vanilla nondairy milk

2 ripe bananas, mashed until smooth

¼ cup vegetable oil

¼ cup maple syrup

Preheat the oven to 375 degrees F. Oil a 9 x 5-inch loaf pan.

Put the flour, wheat germ, baking powder, pumpkin pie spice, and salt in a large bowl and stir with a dry whisk to combine. Add the apples, raisins, cranberries, pecans, and sunflower seeds and stir until coated with the flour. Stir in the nondairy milk, bananas, oil, and maple syrup and mix just until incorporated. The mixture will be quite thick.

Pour the mixture into the prepared pan and smooth the top. Put the pan on a baking sheet and bake for 50 to 60 minutes, until the top is slightly golden and a toothpick inserted in the center comes out clean. If the bread begins to brown too much during the last 15 minutes of baking, tent it with foil.

Put the pan on a wire rack. Let cool for about 15 minutes before removing from the pan and slicing. Serve warm or at room temperature.

Jazzy Tip Using organic whole wheat pastry flour, whole wheat flour, or a combination in place of white flour adds a hearty taste and texture to your baked creations and adds extra nutritional value too!

This rustic, semisweet cornbread is an ideal way to use leftover cooked corn on the cob. A mashed, ripe banana stands in for eggs, while nondairy milk provides the liquid. Serve it alongside chili, soup, or salad, or try it on its own as an afternoon snack.

Double-Corn Cornbread

1¼ cups cornmeal

1 cup whole wheat flour

1 tablespoon baking powder

¼ teaspoon sea salt

⅓ cup brown sugar

Kernels from 1 large ear of corn, cooked, or ¾ cup canned corn kernels, drained

1 cup plain nondairy milk

1 ripe banana, mashed until smooth

¼ cup extra-virgin olive oil

Preheat the oven to 400 degrees F. Oil an 8-inch square baking pan.

Put the cornmeal, flour, baking powder, and salt in a large bowl and stir with a dry whisk to combine. Add the brown sugar and stir with the whisk to combine. Add the corn and stir until coated with the flour. Stir in the nondairy milk, banana, and oil and mix just until incorporated. The mixture will be quite thick.

Pour the mixture into the prepared pan and smooth the top. Bake for 30 to 40 minutes, until slightly golden and a toothpick inserted in the center comes out clean.

Put the pan on a wire rack. Let cool for about 15 minutes before cutting into squares. Serve warm or at room temperature.

Appetizing Starters
and Snacks

Nutritious Nachos, 64

Tasty appetizers make the *perfect start* to any jazzy-licious meal. Whetting guests' palates with various tempting tapas is the ideal way to *welcome company* into your home, and you'll find several recipes in this chapter that fill the bill, from simple dips to elegant artichokes to hearty nachos. If you're really short on time, try pairing crudités, such as carrot and celery sticks and jicama and bell pepper slices, with a bowl of store-bought hummus dip. This easy offering also stands in as a *great afternoon snack.* Speaking of snacks, I think it's important to have a stock of ideas for delicious and nutritious vegan snacks so you won't be tempted by junk food. To that end, I've provided recipes for flavored nuts and homemade trail mix. Or if you're out and about, whether traveling cross-country or running daily errands, take along a piece of fresh fruit, some of your homemade trail mix, or whole-grain tortilla chips, pretzels, or multi-grain crackers.

One summer evening it was my duty to bring the appetizer to a potluck dinner. I was running late and didn't have a plan, but I did have some ripe avocados. Unfortunately, I didn't have lemon juice or lime juice to make guacamole, so I needed to be creative. Thus this easy, breezy dip was born. For a festive presentation, put the bowl of dip in the center of a large platter and surround it with various dippers, such as tortilla chips, crackers, flatbread, or crudités. This dip also makes a wonderful sandwich spread.

Five-Ingredient Guacamole Dip

2 large ripe avocados

1 heaping tablespoon vegan mayonnaise

2 cloves garlic, minced

¼ teaspoon chili powder

⅛ teaspoon sea salt

Put all the ingredients in a medium bowl and mash with a potato masher or large fork until smooth and creamy. Transfer to a serving dish and serve immediately.

This tasty dip is a satisfying appetizer year-round, but it's particularly inviting during the holidays. It truly mimics the texture and taste of traditional pâté. I like to serve this snazzy appetizer with a variety of dippers, such as crudités, pita chips, or whole-grain crackers or flatbread.

Jazzy Vegetarian Not Liver

see photo, page vi   **MAKES 6 TO 8 SERVINGS**

1 tablespoon extra-virgin olive oil, plus more if needed

3 onions, chopped

1 can (15 ounces) sweet peas, drained

¾ cup chopped walnuts

4 ounces firm regular tofu, drained and cubed

2 tablespoons tomato paste

¼ teaspoon sea salt

Freshly ground pepper

Heat 1 tablespoon of the oil in a large skillet over medium-low heat. Add the onions and cook, stirring occasionally, until very tender and lightly browned, about 25 minutes, adding more oil or water, 1 teaspoon at a time, as needed to prevent sticking. Let cool slightly.

Transfer to a food processor. Add the peas, walnuts, tofu, tomato paste, and salt. Process until slightly chunky, stopping to scrape down the sides of the work bowl as needed. (Depending on the size of your food processor, you may need to process the mixture in batches.)

Season with pepper to taste. Spoon the mixture into a serving bowl. Cover tightly and refrigerate for about 4 hours before serving to allow the flavors to blend.

I love to serve this attractive and refreshing starter on hot summer evenings or at an elegant luncheon. It makes great party fare, as both components can be prepared up to a day in advance and the artichokes are so attractive.

Chilled Artichokes with Dill Sauce

DILL DIPPING SAUCE

½ cup vegan mayonnaise

2 to 3 teaspoons freshly squeezed lemon juice

1½ teaspoons chopped fresh dill, or
½ teaspoon dried dill weed

ARTICHOKES

½ onion, sliced

1 tablespoon balsamic, cider, or red wine vinegar

4 artichokes, trimmed
(see note)

To make the dipping sauce, put the mayonnaise, lemon juice to taste, and dill in a small bowl and stir until thoroughly combined. Cover tightly and refrigerate for 2 to 24 hours to allow the flavors to blend.

To prepare the artichokes, put 3 to 4 inches of water in a deep saucepan large enough to hold all the artichokes snugly so they remain upright as they cook. Add the onion and vinegar. Put the artichokes in the pan and bring to a boil over medium-high heat. Decrease the heat to medium, cover, and cook for 25 to 30 minutes, until the artichokes are tender, rotating them halfway through the cooking time. They are done when an outer leaf peels off easily.

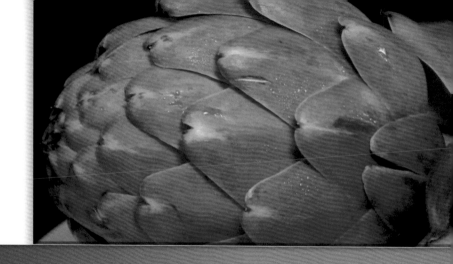

Drain and let cool. Cover and refrigerate for 4 to 24 hours.

Just before serving, slice the artichokes in half vertically. Scoop out the fuzzy center choke with a teaspoon. Put the artichokes on individual salad plates, then put a heaping tablespoon of the sauce in each cavity.

NOTE: To trim and clean artichokes, cut off the top ½ to 1 inch of each artichoke to remove the spiky tips. Cut off any remaining spiky tips with kitchen shears. Trim away the tough edges of the stem. Put the artichokes in a large bowl and cover with cold salted water. Soak for 2 to 3 minutes. Rinse each artichoke under cold water, spreading the leaves to rinse out any residual dirt or sand.

In addition to being a popular starter, this colorful dish can stand in as a quick, fun lunch for kids and adults alike. Plus, the tomatoes and bell peppers help sneak in a serving of veggies, making this zippy dish a real winner.

Nutritious Nachos

MAKES 2 TO 4 SERVINGS

8 to 10 ounces whole-grain tortilla chips

2 cups (1 pint) cherry or grape tomatoes, halved

½ green bell pepper, chopped

½ orange or red bell pepper, chopped

10 large green or black olives, pitted and sliced

2 to 3 tablespoons chopped fresh cilantro
or parsley, or 2 to 3 teaspoons dried

Sea salt

10 to 12 ounces shredded vegan cheese

1 jar (12 to 16 ounces) salsa

Preheat the oven to 375 degrees F. Line two large baking sheets with parchment paper.

Spread the chips in a single layer on the lined baking sheets. Put the tomatoes, bell peppers, olives, and cilantro in a medium bowl and stir gently until thoroughly combined. Season with salt to taste. Sprinkle the mixture evenly over the chips, then scatter the vegan cheese evenly over the top.

Bake for 10 to 12 minutes, until the cheese is bubbly and the edges of some of the chips are golden brown, checking frequently during the last few minutes of baking to ensure the chips don't burn. Serve on individual plates with the salsa alongside, or serve on a large platter with the salsa drizzled over the top.

Whether you're hiking a mountain trail, stuck at the office, or out and about running errands, this nutty and fruity combo will provide a quick and healthful pick-me-up.

Homemade Trail Mix

½ cup raisins

½ cup dried cranberries or cherries

½ cup walnuts

½ cup pecans

6 prunes, cut into raisin-sized pieces (optional)

Combine all the ingredients in a medium bowl. Pack individual servings into ziplock bags or small containers. Stored in the refrigerator, the trail mix will keep for 3 to 4 weeks.

These simple but tasty walnuts are especially welcome during the winter holidays and are a great alternative to heavily sugared snack nuts or candy. Offer them along with an array of appetizers, or just munch on them for an afternoon snack.

Maple-Glazed Walnuts

2 cups walnut halves

2 tablespoons maple syrup

1 tablespoon vegan margarine

Put the walnuts in a medium bowl. Put the maple syrup and margarine in a small saucepan over medium-low heat and cook until the margarine is melted. Stir well, then pour the mixture over the walnuts and toss to coat. Cover and refrigerate for at least 4 hours. Stored in an airtight container in the refrigerator, the walnuts will keep for about 3 weeks.

These delectable almonds, bursting with an almost addictive sweet-salty flavor, are a great substitute for cocktail peanuts or mixed nuts.

Tamari Almonds

3½ cups (1 pound) **raw almonds**
1 to 2 tablespoons **brown sugar**
2 teaspoons **reduced-sodium tamari**

Preheat the oven to 375 degrees F. Line a large, rimmed baking sheet with parchment paper.

Spread the almonds in a single layer on the lined baking sheet. Bake for 4 to 8 minutes, until slightly golden, checking every few minutes to prevent burning.

Transfer to a large bowl. Sprinkle with the brown sugar and tamari and stir until the almonds are evenly coated. Let cool before serving. Stored in an airtight container in the refrigerator, the almonds will keep for about 3 weeks.

Note: If you prefer a saltier taste, add 1 to 2 more teaspoons of tamari as desired.

Jazzy Tip For a delicious nibble anytime, spread peanut butter on apple slices or organic celery sticks. It's a great snack for kids and adults alike. Another fun treat for kids is whole-grain toast spread with peanut butter and topped with sliced banana.

Satisfying Soups and Sandwiches

Avocado Rolls with Sunflower Seeds, 88

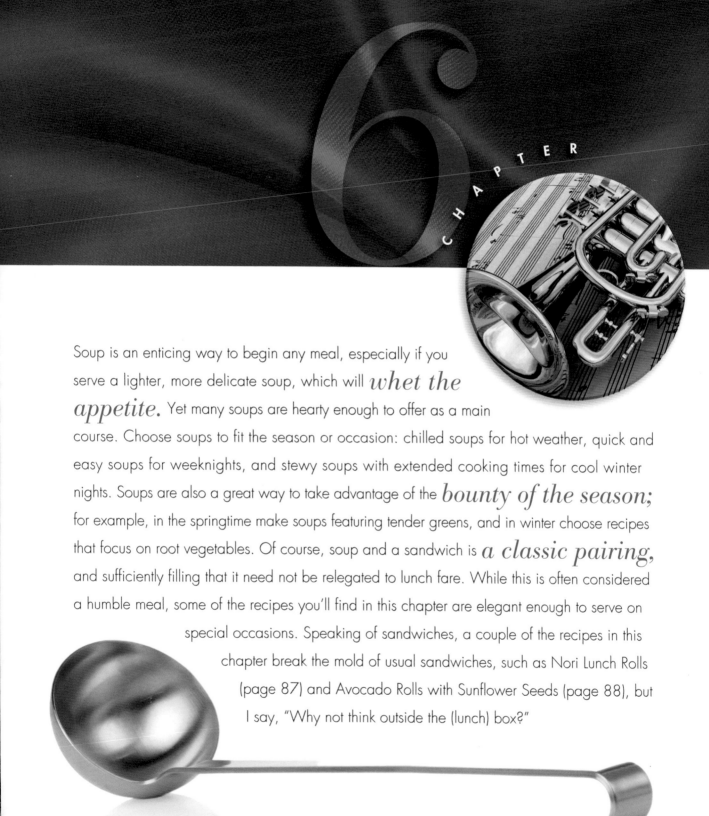

Soup is an enticing way to begin any meal, especially if you serve a lighter, more delicate soup, which will *whet the appetite.* Yet many soups are hearty enough to offer as a main course. Choose soups to fit the season or occasion: chilled soups for hot weather, quick and easy soups for weeknights, and stewy soups with extended cooking times for cool winter nights. Soups are also a great way to take advantage of the *bounty of the season;* for example, in the springtime make soups featuring tender greens, and in winter choose recipes that focus on root vegetables. Of course, soup and a sandwich is *a classic pairing,* and sufficiently filling that it need not be relegated to lunch fare. While this is often considered a humble meal, some of the recipes you'll find in this chapter are elegant enough to serve on special occasions. Speaking of sandwiches, a couple of the recipes in this chapter break the mold of usual sandwiches, such as Nori Lunch Rolls (page 87) and Avocado Rolls with Sunflower Seeds (page 88), but I say, "Why not think outside the (lunch) box?"

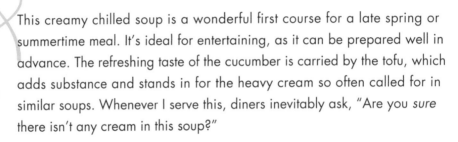

This creamy chilled soup is a wonderful first course for a late spring or summertime meal. It's ideal for entertaining, as it can be prepared well in advance. The refreshing taste of the cucumber is carried by the tofu, which adds substance and stands in for the heavy cream so often called for in similar soups. Whenever I serve this, diners inevitably ask, "Are you *sure* there isn't any cream in this soup?"

Cool Cucumber Soup

MAKES 4 SERVINGS

2 cucumbers

12 ounces soft regular or silken tofu, drained and cubed

½ sweet onion, chopped

2 tablespoons freshly squeezed lemon juice

1 to 2 cloves garlic, chopped

1 teaspoon brown sugar

1 teaspoon dried dill weed, or 1 tablespoon chopped fresh dill, plus more for garnish

Sea salt

Freshly ground pepper

Cut 4 thin slices of cucumber and set aside for the garnish. Peel, seed, and chop the remaining cucumbers.

Put the chopped cucumbers, tofu, onion, lemon juice, garlic, brown sugar and ¼ teaspoon of the dill weed in a blender and process until creamy. Transfer to a bowl and stir in the remaining dill weed. Season with salt and pepper to taste. Cover and refrigerate for 4 to 6 hours.

About 30 minutes before serving, chill four soup bowls. To serve, ladle the soup into the chilled bowls. Garnish each bowl with a cucumber slice topped with a sprinkling of dill weed. Serve immediately.

VARIATION: For a hearty option that's a terrific warm-weather entrée, serve the soup in edible bread bowls. Use a very small, round loaf of crusty bread for each bowl. Slice a ½-inch layer off the top and scoop out the inside of the loaf to form a bowl, leaving about 1 inch of bread along the sides and bottom. Fill with the soup and serve immediately.

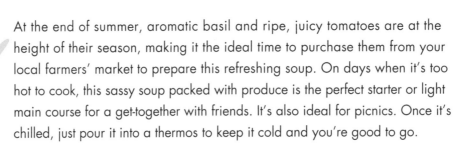

At the end of summer, aromatic basil and ripe, juicy tomatoes are at the height of their season, making it the ideal time to purchase them from your local farmers' market to prepare this refreshing soup. On days when it's too hot to cook, this sassy soup packed with produce is the perfect starter or light main course for a get-together with friends. It's also ideal for picnics. Once it's chilled, just pour it into a thermos to keep it cold and you're good to go.

Garden Vegetable Gazpacho

MAKES 4 TO 6 SERVINGS

4 ripe tomatoes, quartered

4 stalks celery, with leaves, coarsely chopped

1 small onion, quartered

⅓ cup fresh flat-leaf parsley, lightly packed

¼ cup fresh basil leaves, lightly packed

2 tablespoons red wine vinegar

2 tablespoons extra-virgin olive oil, plus more for garnish

1 teaspoon chili powder

1 teaspoon brown sugar (optional)

1 teaspoon reduced-sodium tamari

1 clove garlic

Sea salt

Several grinds freshly ground pepper

Chopped fresh basil, for garnish

Put the tomatoes, celery, onion, parsley, basil leaves, vinegar, oil, chili powder, optional brown sugar, tamari, and garlic in a large bowl and stir to combine. Put half of the mixture in a blender and process until slightly chunky. Pour into a large bowl or pitcher. Repeat with the remaining mixture, then stir the two batches together. Season with salt and pepper to taste. Refrigerate for 4 to 12 hours before serving.

About 30 minutes before serving, chill four to six bowls or mugs. To serve, ladle the gazpacho into the chilled bowls. Garnish with a bit of chopped basil and a drizzle of olive oil if desired. Serve immediately.

NOTE: For a low-fat version of this gazpacho, omit the olive oil.

Top right: Velvety Carrot Soup, page 78; *bottom right:* Cool Cucumber Soup, page 70

This refreshing chilled soup is a welcome first course on a hot day and also substantial enough to serve as a main dish. Blending avocado and tofu together creates a creamy texture, while the parsley contributes a fresh taste and stunning green color. Be sure to make this soup at least three hours ahead of time so it has plenty of time to chill before serving.

Green Goddess Summer Soup

14 to 16 ounces soft regular or silken tofu, drained

½ cup unsweetened nondairy milk

1 avocado

⅓ small sweet onion, chopped

⅓ cup fresh parsley, thick stems removed, lightly packed

4 to 6 fresh basil leaves

2 teaspoons brown sugar

2 teaspoons extra-virgin olive oil (optional)

1 teaspoon balsamic or red wine vinegar

1 teaspoon freshly squeezed lemon juice

¼ teaspoon sea salt

⅛ teaspoon cayenne

1 clove garlic

Chopped fresh parsley, for garnish

Put the tofu, nondairy milk, avocado, onion, parsley, basil, brown sugar, optional oil, vinegar, lemon juice, garlic, salt, and cayenne in a blender. Process until smooth and creamy. If the soup is too thick, add a small amount of water, 1 tablespoon at a time, to achieve the desired consistency, pulsing or blending briefly after each addition. Pour the soup into a large bowl. Cover and refrigerate for 3 to 6 hours.

About 30 minutes before serving, chill two or three soup bowls. To serve, ladle the soup into the chilled bowls. Garnish with a bit of chopped parsley. Serve immediately.

This light, tasty soup is wonderfully simple and an excellent way to feature baby bok choy. To round out the meal, serve it with Nori Lunch Rolls (page 87).

Bok Choy and Penne Soup

4 cups vegetable broth

1½ cups whole-grain penne

1 bunch baby bok choy, thinly sliced

1 to 2 teaspoons light miso

Put the broth in a medium saucepan over medium-high heat and bring to a boil. Stir in the penne and bok choy. Decrease the heat to medium-low, cover, and simmer, stirring occasionally, until the penne is tender but firm, 10 to 12 minutes. Remove from the heat. Ladle about ¼ cup of the liquid into a small bowl, add the miso, and stir until well combined. Stir the miso mixture into the soup and serve immediately.

Served with whole-grain crackers or crusty rolls, this light soup makes a great first course or light supper. Orzo is a rice-shaped pasta that cooks up quickly, making it excellent for adding body to soups.

Carrot and Orzo Soup

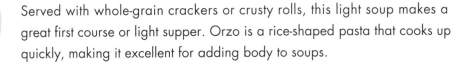

MAKES 4 SERVINGS

4 cups vegetable broth

½ cup water

1 large carrot, diced

1 scallion, white and green parts, sliced

1 tablespoon chopped fresh flat-leaf parsley, plus more for garnish

1 teaspoon reduced-sodium tamari

¾ cup orzo, preferably multicolored

Sea salt

Freshly ground pepper

Put the broth and water in a medium saucepan over medium-high heat and bring to a boil. Stir in the carrot, scallion, parsley, and tamari. Decrease the heat to medium-low, cover, and simmer for about 8 minutes. Stir in the orzo and simmer, stirring occasionally, until the orzo and carrots are tender, about 10 minutes. Season with salt and pepper to taste. To serve, ladle the soup into bowls. Garnish with parsley if desired.

I like to make this soup as a quick one-pot meal when time is at a premium. Because it includes lettuce and tofu, gently simmered in vegetable broth, you could say it incorporates salad, protein, and soup, all in one delectable dish. Smoked or baked tofu ups the flavor factor, but in a pinch you can also use firm regular tofu.

Penne and Lettuce Soup

MAKES 3 TO 4 SERVINGS

4 cups vegetable broth

1 cup whole-grain penne

3 ounces smoked or baked tofu, cubed

½ teaspoon ground turmeric

2 cups thinly sliced romaine lettuce

Sea salt

Freshly ground black pepper

Put the broth in a medium saucepan over medium-high heat and bring to a boil. Stir in the penne, tofu, and turmeric. Decrease the heat to medium-low, cover, and simmer, stirring occasionally, until the penne is tender but firm, 8 to 10 minutes. Stir in the lettuce and simmer just until it wilts but is still bright green, about 1 minute. Season with salt and pepper to taste. Serve immediately.

I love to serve this stunning, colorful soup as an elegant first course on a chilly night. However, it is also delicious served cold, making it suitable for any time of year. The vegetables are blended to produce a thick, smooth soup that's low in calories and high in nutrition. It's very tasty as is, but if you make it a day in advance and store it tightly covered in the refrigerator, the flavors will meld and develop even more. Just note that you may need to add a bit more broth or nondairy milk if you reheat the soup.

Velvety Carrot Soup

MAKES 4 TO 6 SERVINGS

5 large carrots, peeled and coarsely chopped

3 medium white potatoes, peeled and coarsely chopped

1 cup unsweetened nondairy milk, plus more as needed

1 cup vegetable broth, plus more as needed

1 teaspoon brown sugar

1 teaspoon italian seasoning

½ teaspoon reduced-sodium tamari

Sea salt

Freshly ground pepper

2 tablespoons chopped fresh parsley, for garnish

Steam the carrots and potatoes until soft but not mushy, about 10 minutes. Transfer to a large bowl. Add the nondairy milk, broth, brown sugar, italian seasoning, and tamari and stir to combine.

Put half of the mixture in a blender and process until smooth. Pour into a soup pot. Repeat with the remaining mixture, then stir the two batches together.

Put the pot over medium-low heat and simmer, stirring often, until heated through, about 10 minutes, adding more broth or nondairy milk to achieve the desired consistency. Season with salt and pepper to taste. To serve, ladle the soup into bowls. Garnish with the parsley if desired.

Jazzy Tip A report from the United Nations pegs livestock as being responsible for 18 percent of greenhouse gases—a greater percentage than that attributable to cars, planes, and other forms of transport that use fossil fuels. And producing a single liter of cow's milk requires a whopping 990 liters of water.

Celery is often relegated to hiding away in the base of a soup, but this recipe highlights its faintly bitter taste and trademark crunchy texture front and center. The soup is balanced with root vegetables for heft, tofu for protein, and turmeric for its golden color and distinctive flavor. The end result is a soup hearty and nutritious enough to serve as a main course, especially if accompanied by a crisp green salad and crusty whole-grain bread or brown rice.

Celery, Carrot, and Tofu Soup

MAKES 4 TO 6 SERVINGS

6 cups vegetable broth

2 cups water, plus more as needed

1 bunch celery, with leaves, chopped

4 large potatoes, peeled and chopped

5 large carrots, chopped

¼ cup chopped fresh parsley

8 cloves garlic, chopped

1 teaspoon italian seasoning or other all-purpose seasoning blend

½ teaspoon ground turmeric

14 to 16 ounces firm regular tofu, drained and cubed

1 teaspoon reduced-sodium tamari

6 stalks asparagus, chopped

Sea salt

Freshly ground pepper

Put the broth, water, celery, potatoes, carrots, parsley, garlic, italian seasoning, and turmeric in a large soup pot over medium-high heat. Add more water as needed to just cover the vegetables. Bring to a boil. Decrease the heat to medium-low, cover, and simmer, stirring occasionally, for about 40 minutes.

Meanwhile, put the tofu in a medium bowl and drizzle with the tamari. Toss to coat.

Add the tofu and asparagus to the pot and simmer, stirring occasionally, until the tofu is heated through and the asparagus is tender, about 10 minutes. Season with salt and pepper to taste. Serve piping hot.

Low in fat and calories and chock-full of nutrients, this is a great go-to one-pot meal. That said, you can't go wrong serving whole-grain crackers and a leafy green salad with this simple yet savory soup.

Simple Veggie Soup

4 cups vegetable broth

2 medium sweet potatoes, peeled and chopped

6 stalks celery, with leaves, chopped

3 carrots, chopped

½ head cauliflower, cut into small florets

1 large white potato, peeled and chopped

1 onion, chopped

½ cup chopped fresh parsley

Sea salt

Freshly ground pepper

Put the broth, sweet potatoes, celery, carrots, cauliflower, potato, onion, and parsley in a large soup pot and bring to a boil over medium-high heat. Decrease the heat to medium-low, cover, and simmer, stirring occasionally, until the vegetables are tender and the flavors have melded, 45 to 55 minutes. Season with salt and pepper to taste. Serve piping hot.

This is a great main dish soup for a simple winter supper, and one of my most popular recipes. Sweet potatoes provide excellent nutritional value and beautiful color, along with a pleasing contrast to the earthiness of the mushrooms and brightness of the green beans.

Savory Sweet Potato Soup

1 tablespoon extra-virgin olive oil

2 red onions, chopped

1 large stalk celery, with leaves, chopped

8 ounces cremini or white button mushrooms, chopped

3 cloves garlic, minced

1 teaspoon brown sugar (optional)

1 teaspoon reduced-sodium tamari

8 cups vegetable broth

1½ cups water, plus more as needed

3 large sweet potatoes, peeled and cubed

2 medium white potatoes, cubed

2 cups cut fresh green beans, in bite-sized pieces

1 parsnip, sliced

Sea salt

Freshly ground pepper

Heat the oil in a soup pot over medium heat. Add the onions and cook, stirring occasionally, until slightly softened, about 5 minutes. Add the celery and cook, stirring occasionally, until tender, about 8 minutes. Add the mushrooms and cook, stirring occasionally and adding a bit of water as needed to prevent sticking, until tender, about 8 minutes. Add the garlic, optional brown sugar, and tamari and cook, stirring occasionally, until the onions are golden, about 5 minutes. Stir in the broth, water, sweet potatoes, potatoes, green beans, and parsnip, adding more water as needed to just cover the vegetables. Decrease the heat to medium-low, cover, and simmer, stirring occasionally, until the vegetables are soft and the flavors have melded, about 1 hour. Season with salt and pepper to taste. Serve piping hot.

Jazzy Tip To decrease the fat content in many savory dishes, you can replace some or all of the oil used in stovetop cooking with vegetable broth or water. Use 2 to 3 tablespoons of either broth or water to replace 1 tablespoon of oil. Unlike oil, these liquids will evaporate during cooking, so be watchful and add more as needed.

With its bounty of root vegetables, this warming soup is a great choice during the winter months. For other times of the year, feel free to substitute your favorite seasonal veggies and adjust the cooking time accordingly. Because it makes a large amount, you can get several lunches or dinners out of this recipe. Crusty whole-grain bread is the perfect accompaniment.

Warming Winter Soup

6 stalks celery, with leaves, chopped

1 sweet onion, chopped

1 teaspoon italian seasoning or other herb blend

8 cups vegetable broth

1 teaspoon reduced-sodium tamari

3 cups water, plus more as needed

2 medium sweet potatoes, peeled and chopped

5 medium red potatoes, peeled and chopped

5 carrots, chopped

2 cups chopped green beans

6 large cremini or white button mushrooms, sliced

1 can (15 ounces) white beans, drained and rinsed

Sea salt

Freshly ground pepper

Put the celery, onion, italian seasoning, and ¼ cup of the broth in a large soup pot over medium heat. Cook, stirring occasionally, until the onion is translucent, about 8 minutes, adding more broth as needed, 1 tablespoon at a time, if the mixture becomes dry. Stir in the tamari and cook, stirring occasionally, until the celery and onion are tender, about 8 minutes. Stir in the remaining broth, the water, sweet potatoes, red potatoes, carrots, green beans, and mushrooms. Decrease the heat, cover, and simmer, stirring occasionally, for 30 minutes. Stir in the white beans and simmer until the vegetables are tender, 15 to 20 minutes longer, adding more water as needed to achieve the desired consistency. Season with salt and pepper to taste. Serve piping hot.

Jazzy Tip When dining out, always ask that your food be made without any animal products. Ask your server to make sure that no eggs, dairy products, or broth made from chicken, beef, or fish are being used in anything you order, such as in your "vegetable" soup or pasta "primavera."

I'm always on the lookout for midday foods that I can prepare in ten minutes or less, and this satisfying sandwich fills the bill. The salty tang of the miso pairs with the mashed avocado and chili powder to make a sandwich that's full of flavor, not to mention nutrition.

Avocado Open-Faced Sandwiches

MAKES 2 SERVINGS

4 slices sprouted whole-grain bread

1 large avocado

¼ to ½ teaspoon chili powder

¼ teaspoon sea salt

2 teaspoons light miso

¾ to 1½ ounces (1 to 2 cups, lightly packed) mixed baby greens

Toast the bread if you wish. Put the avocado, chili powder, and salt in a small bowl and mash with a fork until smooth and thoroughly combined.

Spread ½ teaspoon of the miso on one side of each slice of bread. Spread one-quarter of the avocado mixture in an even layer over each slice. Top with one-quarter of the baby greens. Serve open-faced.

These sandwiches taste so much like the traditional version that they take me right back to my childhood in Ohio, where I often ordered a reuben sandwich at the local deli. To re-create the experience in your own home, pair this sandwich with Zesty Zucchini Oven Fries (page 163) or Fabulous Oven Fries (page 162) and dill pickle spears.

Reuben-Style Sandwiches

MAKES 2 SANDWICHES

THOUSAND ISLAND DRESSING

¼ cup vegan mayonnaise

1 tablespoon sweet pickle relish

1 tablespoon catsup

2 teaspoons minced scallion, white and green parts

SANDWICHES

1 cup sauerkraut

2 teaspoons vegan margarine

4 slices rye bread

6 slices vegan swiss cheese

6 slices vegan canadian bacon or ham

To make the dressing, put all the ingredients in a small bowl and whisk until thoroughly combined.

To make the sandwiches, set a colander in the sink. Put the sauerkraut in the colander and press firmly with your hands or the back of a wooden spoon to extract as much moisture as possible. Spread ½ teaspoon of the margarine evenly over one side of each slice of bread. Place 2 of the slices, margarine-side down, in a large skillet. Top each with 3 slices of vegan cheese, 3 slices of vegan canadian bacon, and half of the sauerkraut. Spoon 1 to 2 tablespoons of the dressing over the sauerkraut and top with another slice of bread, margarine-side up.

Weigh down the sandwiches with a heavy lid or sandwich weight. Cook over medium-low heat until the underside is brown and crispy, about 5 minutes. Flip the sandwiches and cook until the other side is brown and crispy and the vegan cheese is oozing. Serve immediately.

NOTE: The Thousand Island Dressing is sensational on salads, so that's a great use for any leftovers. Stored in an airtight container in the refrigerator, leftover dressing will keep for about 5 days.

TEMPEH REUBEN SANDWICHES: If you'd rather not use a meat analog in this recipe, you can substitute sautéed tempeh. Cut an 8- to 10-ounce piece of tempeh in half horizontally, then into 4 slices vertically. Heat 1 tablespoon of extra-virgin olive oil in a medium skillet over medium heat. Put the tempeh in the skillet and sprinkle with 1 to 2 teaspoons of reduced-sodium tamari. Cover and cook for 3 to 5 minutes, until the underside is golden. Flip each slice and cook until the other side is golden. Proceed with the recipe as directed, replacing the vegan canadian bacon with 2 slices of tempeh per sandwich.

I love the vegetable nori rolls that my local Japanese restaurant serves and wanted to come up with something similar that I could easily make at home. The result is this rustic roll that doesn't require a bamboo sushi mat—or extensive sushi-rolling experience. High-quality toasted nori sheets are available at most natural food stores.

Nori Lunch Rolls

MAKES 2 SERVINGS

2 sheets toasted nori

2 heaping teaspoons vegan mayonnaise

1 avocado, cut into thin strips

1 carrot, cut lengthwise into 6 thin strips

½ cucumber, peeled, seeded, and cut lengthwise into 4 or 6 thin strips

¾ ounce (1 cup, lightly packed) **mixed baby greens** (optional)

1 teaspoon light miso

Reduced-sodium tamari, for dipping (optional)

Lay a nori sheet on a large cutting board with the long side running horizontally. Spread half of the vegan mayonnaise in a 1-inch strip across the nori sheet about 2 inches from the bottom edge. Evenly arrange half of the avocado, carrot, cucumber, and optional greens atop the mayonnaise. Spread ½ teaspoon of the miso in a thin line along the top edge of the nori sheet. (It will hold the roll together once it's rolled up.)

Starting at the bottom edge, roll the nori tightly and evenly around the vegetables. Gently but firmly press the edge to seal the roll. Set the roll seam-side down and cut it crosswise into 3 or 4 pieces (a sharp serrated knife works best). Repeat to make the second roll. Serve immediately, with the optional tamari alongside in a small bowl.

These versatile roll-ups are perfect for any midday meal, from a casual brunch to an elegant luncheon. They also travel well, making them ideal for packed lunches or picnics. Just wrap them in parchment paper and go!

Avocado Rolls with Sunflower Seeds

MAKES 2 SERVINGS

2 whole-grain flour tortillas or wraps

¼ cup store-bought hummus

2 tablespoons vegan mayonnaise

4 ounces (5 cups, lightly packed) **mixed baby greens**

1 avocado, sliced

8 small green or black olives, pitted and chopped (optional)

2 teaspoons raw or unsalted roasted sunflower seeds

Lay the tortillas on a large cutting board. Spread half of the hummus evenly over half of each tortilla. Spread half of the vegan mayonnaise evenly over the other half of each tortilla. Evenly arrange half of the greens, avocado, optional olives, and sunflower seeds over the lower two-thirds of each wrap.

Starting at the bottom edge, roll the tortilla tightly and evenly around the filling. Gently but firmly press the edge to seal the roll. Set the roll seam-side down and cut it diagonally into 5 or 6 pieces. To serve, place the pieces on a plate cut-side down.

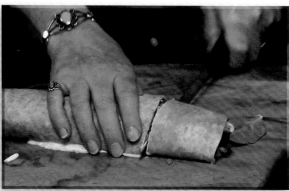

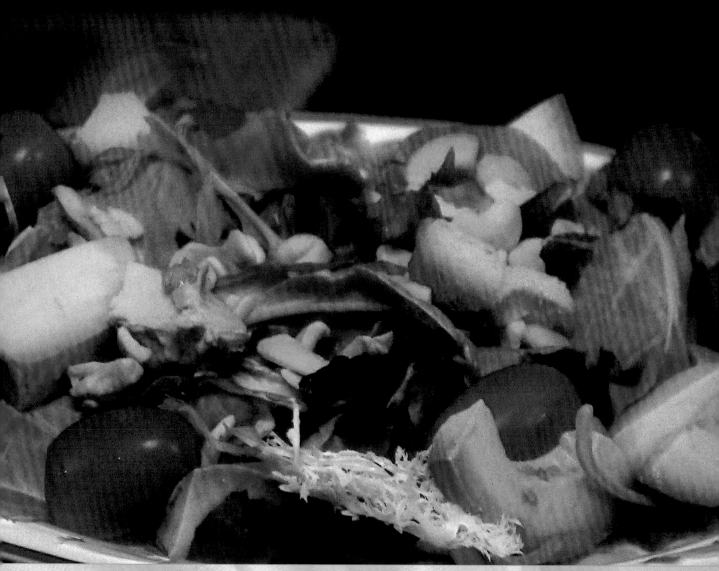

Sassy Salads

Avocado-Cashew Salad, 96

A crisp green salad is a *refreshing* and *nutritious* way to round out any savory meal. Or, with the addition of ingredients like avocados, nuts, seeds, tempeh, or tofu, a salad can become the meal. These types of ingredients will add protein, healthful fats, rich flavors, and contrasting textures to your daily greens. I love to use *unexpected ingredients,* such as figs, raisins, or dried cranberries, to add *a touch of sweetness.* Salads are a natural in summertime, when so many types of produce are in season. But because various greens are available year-round, they can also *provide spark* and a bit of *welcome freshness* in the wintertime.

This simple fruit salad is great as a side dish for breakfast or brunch, or try serving it as a refreshing first course or light dessert option for lunch or supper. The combination of orange cantaloupe, red watermelon, and dark blueberries is as attractive as it is flavorful, so for the best effect, present it in a glass bowl.

Fancy Fruit Salad

2 to 3 cups cubed cantaloupe
2 to 3 cups cubed watermelon
1 cup fresh blueberries
Basil sprigs, for garnish

Put the cantaloupe, watermelon, and blueberries in a large bowl and stir gently until thoroughly combined. Serve chilled or at room temperature, garnished with the basil sprigs if desired.

During the summer months when basil is growing like crazy on my back deck and Jersey tomatoes fresh off the vine are plentiful at my local farmers' market, I like to make this straightforward salad. Sometimes just a few simple ingredients produce a very flavorful dish, as this combination of the best of summer's bounty proves.

Summer Tomato Salad with Basil

MAKES 4 SERVINGS

4 large ripe tomatoes, chopped

10 to 12 large fresh basil leaves, minced

1 tablespoon extra-virgin olive oil,
plus more for drizzling

1 clove garlic, minced

¼ teaspoon sea salt

Freshly ground pepper

Put the tomatoes, basil, oil, garlic, and salt in a large bowl and stir gently until thoroughly combined. Season with pepper to taste. Let sit at room temperature for 15 to 30 minutes to infuse the tomatoes with the flavors of the basil and garlic.

To serve, spoon the salad onto individual plates. Top with a dusting of pepper and a drizzle of olive oil if desired.

NOTE: For a low-fat version of this salad, omit the olive oil. Ripe and juicy summer tomatoes often provide all the "dressing" you need in this recipe!

Jazzy Tip Buying fresh produce from your local farmers' market is the best way to support small farmers and keep the money you spend in your community.

This salad, which features ripe, peak-of-season tomatoes, was inspired by a trip to my local farmers' market. Slices of succulent tomatoes are arranged on a large platter with bright green basil leaves tucked between them. Because the dish can be prepared well in advance and the presentation is so festive, it's perfect for summer parties.

Tomato-Basil Pinwheel

MAKES 4 TO 6 SERVINGS

2 to 3 large ripe tomatoes, sliced

20 to 30 fresh basil leaves

1 tablespoon extra-virgin olive oil

½ teaspoon sea salt

5 or 6 short basil sprigs, for garnish

Place a slice of tomato near the edge of a 10- to 12-inch plate or serving platter. Arrange alternating tomato slices and basil leaves around the perimeter of the platter, overlapping them slightly and spiraling inward to form a pinwheel pattern. Sprinkle with the salt. Drizzle the oil evenly over the top. Cover tightly with plastic wrap and refrigerate up to 2 hours, until serving time.

Garnish with the basil sprigs if desired. Serve immediately.

TOMATO, BASIL, AND TOFU PINWHEEL: For a vegan take on a classic caprese salad, add baked tofu. Cut 8 ounces of store-bought baked tofu into thin slices. Proceed with the recipe as directed, placing the tofu between the tomato slices and basil leaves.

This is my go-to salad when I have company over. The balsamic dressing adds a touch of sophistication to the delicate, sweet taste of the greens. Because the flavors are clean and straightforward, it pairs well with a wide variety of dishes. For an especially elegant first course, serve Warm Bakery Bread with Herbed Dipping Oil (page 170) with the salad.

Mixed Baby Greens Salad

SWEET BALSAMIC DRESSING

¼ cup extra-virgin olive oil

2 tablespoons balsamic vinegar

2 teaspoons brown sugar

1 teaspoon dijon mustard

Sea salt

Freshly ground pepper

SALAD

8 ounces (10 cups, lightly packed) mixed baby greens

20 cherry or grape tomatoes

½ large cucumber, peeled and thinly sliced

4 heaping teaspoons unsalted roasted sunflower seeds or chopped walnuts

To make the dressing, put the oil, vinegar, brown sugar, and mustard in a small bowl and briskly whisk until smooth and emulsified. Season with salt and pepper to taste.

To make the salad, divide the greens among four salad plates. For each serving, top with 5 tomatoes and one-quarter of the cucumber slices. Sprinkle with 1 heaping teaspoon of the sunflower seeds. Drizzle 1 tablespoon of the dressing over each salad. Serve immediately.

NOTE: The dressing makes more than you'll need for this salad, but it's a great basic dressing to have on hand and is used in other recipes in this book. Stored in an airtight container in the refrigerator, leftover dressing will keep for about 1 week. Just whisk it briskly before using.

The generous amounts of avocado and cashews in this salad make it a meal in itself. Try it as a light summertime lunch.

Avocado-Cashew Salad

DRESSING
4 teaspoons flaxseed oil

2 teaspoons extra-virgin olive oil

2 teaspoons balsamic vinegar

SALAD
4 ounces (5 cups, lightly packed) **mixed baby greens**

20 cherry or grape tomatoes, halved

1 red or yellow bell pepper, chopped

½ bermuda onion, chopped

½ cup chopped raw or roasted cashews

1 large avocado, sliced

To make the dressing, put all the ingredients in a small bowl and briskly whisk until smooth and emulsified.

To make the salad, divide the greens between two large salad plates. For each serving, top with half of the tomatoes, bell pepper, onion, and cashews. Arrange the avocado slices on top in a spiral pattern. Drizzle with half of the dressing. Serve immediately.

Jazzy Tip I like to wash my salad greens in the morning or well ahead of my meal. Gently wash the greens, then spin them dry in a salad spinner. Transfer to a large bowl and place a dry paper towel on top of the greens. Cover the bowl with plastic wrap and chill. Your greens will be super crisp and ready to toss into your salad at a moment's notice.

Although the combination may sound unusual, crunchy kale, juicy tomatoes, and sweet figs come together to make a delectable and filling salad. This is an innovative dish that works well as a light luncheon entrée or as an impressive first course.

Fig, Kale, and Tomato Salad

MAKES 2 TO 4 SERVINGS

3 to 4 cups chopped romaine lettuce

1 ripe tomato, chopped

½ cup finely chopped kale

2 large dried figs, stemmed and thinly sliced

2 tablespoons unsalted roasted sunflower seeds

1 to 3 tablespoons Sweet Balsamic Dressing (see page 95)

Put the lettuce, tomato, kale, figs, and sunflower seeds in a large salad bowl. Add the dressing to taste and toss until the greens are evenly coated. Let the salad sit at room temperature for about 20 minutes to soften the kale a bit. Serve at room temperature.

NOTES

- Kale varieties with thinner leaves, such as red russian (also called lacinato or tuscan kale), are best suited for this recipe.
- For a simple alternative dressing, whisk together 1 tablespoon of extra-virgin olive oil and 1 tablespoon of freshly squeezed lemon juice in a small bowl. Season with sea salt to taste.

No doubt about it, potato salad is perennially popular for picnics and summertime meals. For a more rustic version that's also more nutritious, try leaving the skins on the potatoes. This recipe is easily doubled or tripled to feed a crowd.

Country-Style Red Potato Salad

10 to 12 small red potatoes, peeled and cubed

2 large carrots, diced

2 to 3 stalks celery, with leaves, chopped

½ cup sliced green or black olives

½ cup vegan mayonnaise, plus more as needed

1 to 2 tablespoons dijon mustard

2 teaspoons italian seasoning

1 teaspoon brown sugar

½ teaspoon sea salt

½ cup chopped fresh parsley

¼ cup chopped fresh basil (optional)

Freshly ground pepper

Paprika, for dusting

Tomato wedges, for garnish

Dill sprigs, for garnish

Steam the potatoes until tender but still slightly firm, about 8 minutes. Transfer to a large bowl and let cool until slightly warm. Add the carrots, celery, and olives and stir gently until well combined.

Put the vegan mayonnaise, mustard, italian seasoning, brown sugar, and salt in a small bowl and whisk to combine. Add to the potato mixture and stir gently until well combined. Add the parsley, optional basil, and pepper to taste and stir gently until evenly distributed.

Cover and refrigerate for 2 to 12 hours. Check the consistency before serving; if the mixture seems dry, stir in a bit more vegan mayonnaise, 1 tablespoon at a time. To serve, sprinkle paprika over the top. Garnish with tomato wedges and dill sprigs if desired.

Besides displaying a beautiful rainbow of colors, this salad offers a crunchy yet creamy texture and a zesty taste that make it appealing summer fare. Whole-grain crackers are a good accompaniment to this dish.

Avocado and Black Bean Confetti Salad

MAKES 3 TO 4 SERVINGS

DRESSING

2 tablespoons extra-virgin olive oil, flaxseed oil, or a combination

1 tablespoon balsamic vinegar

1 tablespoon chopped fresh cilantro, or 1 teaspoon dried

½ teaspoon sea salt

½ teaspoon chili powder

¼ to ⅛ teaspoon cayenne

⅛ teaspoon freshly ground pepper

SALAD

1 can (15 ounces) black beans, drained and rinsed

½ cucumber, seeded and cubed

1 cup cherry or grape tomatoes, halved

1 red bell pepper, chopped

½ cup chopped red onion

2 cloves garlic, minced

1 avocado, cubed

To make the dressing, put all the ingredients in a small bowl and briskly whisk until smooth and emulsified.

To make the salad, combine the beans, cucumber, tomatoes, bell pepper, onion and garlic in a salad bowl and stir gently until thoroughly combined. Pour the dressing over the salad and stir gently until the vegetables are evenly coated. At this point, the salad may be covered and refrigerated for up to 3 hours if desired. Just before serving, add the avocado and toss gently. Serve immediately.

This salad is a good choice for a first or second course when you're hosting a dinner party, as all the ingredients can be prepared earlier in the day and chilled separately until serving time. You can also compose the individual servings (sans dressing) a few hours in advance. Drizzle the dressing over the salad just before serving.

Walnut, Beet, and Tofu Salad

MAKES 4 TO 6 SERVINGS

4 beets

3 ounces (4 cups, lightly packed) **mixed baby greens**

8 ounces smoked or baked tofu, cubed or sliced

½ **cup chopped walnuts**

4 tablespoons Sweet Balsamic Dressing (see page 95)

Put the beets in a large saucepan, add water to cover, and bring to a boil over medium-high heat. Decrease the heat to medium-low, cover, and cook until easily pierced with a fork, about 25 minutes.

Transfer to a plate using a slotted spoon and let cool. When cool enough to handle, slip off the skins by hand. Cut off the root ends and slice ¼ to ½ inch thick. Put the beets in a bowl, cover, and refrigerate until completely chilled, about 1 hour.

To serve, divide the greens among four salad plates. For each serving, arrange one-quarter of the beet slices atop the greens. Scatter one-quarter of the tofu and walnuts over the beets. Drizzle with about 1 tablespoon of the dressing. Serve immediately.

I like to make this salad ahead of time and serve it well chilled, but it's also tasty at room temperature, right out of the mixing bowl. Turmeric lends this salad a beautiful color and also has impressive health benefits. For a delectable luncheon entrée, serve a scoop of this salad atop mixed baby greens, garnished with cucumber slices and red bell pepper strips, with whole-grain crackers or flatbread on the side.

Eggless Egg Salad

MAKES 3 TO 4 SERVINGS

14 to 16 ounces firm regular tofu, drained

2 tablespoons vegan mayonnaise, plus more as needed

1 heaping tablespoon dijon mustard

1 carrot, diced

1 small stalk celery, diced

2 teaspoons chopped fresh parsley or basil (optional)

½ to 1 teaspoon italian seasoning

¼ teaspoon sea salt

¼ teaspoon ground turmeric

Freshly ground pepper

Put the tofu in a medium bowl and mash with a potato masher or large fork until crumbly. Add the vegan mayonnaise and mustard and mash until well combined and the mixture has the desired consistency. Add the carrot, celery, optional parsley, italian seasoning, salt, and turmeric and stir until thoroughly combined, adding more vegan mayonnaise, 1 teaspoon at a time, as needed to achieve the desired consistency. Season with pepper to taste. Serve chilled or at room temperature.

NOTE: This salad makes a super sandwich filling. Use whole-grain bread spread with vegan mayonnaise or mustard or both. Add romaine lettuce or sprouts and sliced tomato. Serve the sandwiches with dill pickle spears and sweet potato chips on the side if you like.

Perfect Pastas

Quick Lasagna Rolls, 120

CHAPTER 8

Nothing showcases the *simple pleasures* of vegan cuisine better than a satisfying pasta dish. I adore pasta in all shapes and sizes and cook up pasta meals on a regular basis. They are *easy, economical, filling, and delicious.* Just steam mixed veggies and toss them with cooked penne. Sauté greens with olive oil and garlic and toss them with cooked fusilli. Heat up a jar of marinara sauce and frozen green beans and toss them with cooked spaghetti. Chop *tomatoes, garlic, olives, and basil* and toss them with cooked farfalle. Both my mom and my grandma made lots of spaghetti, lasagna, and macaroni when I was a kid, and the craving has stuck with me. If you *love pasta,* this is the chapter for you!

This supremely fresh-tasting pasta is perfect summer fare. The steaming hot pasta cooks the tomatoes just enough to ensure that they're bursting with flavor. I love to make this for company because most of the prep can be done beforehand and the colorful combination of veggies makes for an attractive presentation.

Arugula, Artichoke, and Tomato Penne

MAKES 4 SERVINGS

1 pound whole-grain penne or other pasta

2 ripe tomatoes, chopped

10 to 15 leaves fresh basil, very thinly sliced

1 clove garlic, minced

1 teaspoon fines herbes or other herb blend

½ teaspoon sea salt

Several grinds freshly ground pepper

2 tablespoons extra-virgin olive oil

1 bunch arugula (about 4 ounces), cleaned and stemmed

1 jar (6 ounces) marinated artichoke hearts, drained

Bring a large pot of salted water to a boil over medium-high heat. Stir in the penne. Decrease the heat to medium-low and cook, stirring occasionally, until tender but firm.

Meanwhile, put the tomatoes, basil, garlic, fines herbes, salt, and pepper in a bowl large enough to also accommodate the cooked penne. Stir gently until well combined. Drizzle in 1 tablespoon of the oil and stir gently until the tomatoes are evenly coated. Coarsely chop the arugula and put it on top of the tomato mixture. Chop the artichoke hearts and put them in a small bowl.

Drain the penne well and, while it is still piping hot, pour it over the tomato mixture. Drizzle with the remaining tablespoon of oil and toss gently until thoroughly combined. Gently stir in the artichoke hearts. Serve immediately.

NOTE: The tomato mixture and artichokes may be prepared up to 4 hours in advance. Just store them separately in covered bowls in the refrigerator.

Lettuce sauce may sound crazy, but it truly isn't. The hot pasta heats the lettuce and tomatoes just enough to bring out their flavors, producing a full-bodied sauce with a fresh, zingy taste. The entire dish takes only about fifteen minutes to prepare, making this the perfect entrée when time is at a premium.

Rigatoni with Lettuce Sauce

MAKES 4 SERVINGS

1 pound whole-grain rigatoni, spaghetti, or other pasta

2 cups (about 1 pint) cherry or grape tomatoes, halved

1 small head romaine lettuce, coarsely chopped

3 tablespoons chopped fresh basil, or 1 teaspoon dried

¼ cup walnuts, chopped

8 large green olives, preferably queen or sevillano, pitted and diced

1 tablespoon extra-virgin olive oil, plus more if needed

2 cloves garlic, minced

Pinch cayenne (optional)

Sea salt

Freshly ground pepper

Bring a large pot of salted water to a boil over medium-high heat. Stir in the rigatoni. Decrease the heat to medium-low and cook, stirring occasionally, until tender but firm.

Meanwhile, put the tomatoes in a bowl large enough to also accommodate the rigatoni. Lightly mash with a potato masher to release some of their juices. Add the lettuce, basil, walnuts, olives, 1 tablespoon of the oil, the garlic, and optional cayenne. Stir until well combined.

Drain the rigatoni well and, while it is still piping hot, pour it over the tomato mixture. Toss gently until everything is thoroughly combined and the lettuce is wilted, adding additional oil if the mixture seems dry. Season with salt and pepper to taste. Serve immediately.

This nutritious and delicious pasta dish, which can be prepared in only fifteen minutes, truly is a one-pot meal, making it a great weeknight supper. The wheat germ stands in well for parmesan cheese. It also helps hold the ingredients together and adds texture and flavor.

Quick Penne with Broccoli and Sun-Dried Tomatoes

1 pound whole-grain penne or other pasta

1 large bunch broccoli, cut into bite-size florets

1 jar (8 ounces) oil-packed sun-dried tomatoes, drained and chopped

1 to 2 tablespoons extra-virgin olive oil

12 large leaves fresh basil, very thinly sliced, or 2 teaspoons dried

¼ teaspoon garlic powder

¼ cup toasted wheat germ

Sea salt

Freshly ground pepper

Bring a large pot of salted water to a boil over medium-high heat. Stir in the penne. Decrease the heat to medium-low and cook, stirring occasionally, until the penne is almost tender. Add the broccoli and cook, stirring occasionally, until the penne is tender but firm and the broccoli is crisp-tender, 3 to 4 minutes.

Meanwhile, put the sun-dried tomatoes, 1 tablespoon of the oil, and the basil and garlic powder in a bowl large enough to also accommodate the penne and broccoli and stir until well combined.

Drain the penne and broccoli well and, while they are still piping hot, pour them over the tomato mixture. Add the wheat germ and toss gently until thoroughly combined. Add more oil as desired, season with salt and pepper to taste, and toss again. Serve immediately.

Arugula adds a peppery bite to this pesto without overwhelming the flavors of the other ingredients, and the wheat germ adds extra nutrition and a subtle crunch. This recipe is among my top warm-weather go-to dishes because it is special enough to serve to guests yet is also quick to prepare and doesn't heat up the kitchen. Serve it with crusty whole-grain bread and a simple romaine salad for a satisfying meal.

Arugula-and-Walnut Pesto Pasta

1 pound whole-grain pasta

2¼ ounces (3 cups, lightly packed) **baby arugula**

1 cup fresh basil, lightly packed

1 cup chopped walnuts

⅔ cup extra-virgin olive oil

¼ cup toasted wheat germ

2 tablespoons water

2 cloves garlic

¼ teaspoon sea salt

Freshly ground pepper

3 small tomatoes, cut into wedges

Bring a large pot of salted water to a boil over medium-high heat. Stir in the pasta. Decrease the heat to medium-low and cook, stirring occasionally, until tender but firm.

Meanwhile put the arugula, basil, walnuts, oil, wheat germ, water, garlic, and salt in a blender or food processor. Process until smooth, stopping to scrape down the sides of the blender jar or work bowl as needed. (Depending on the size of your blender or food processor, you may need to process the mixture in batches.) Season with pepper to taste.

Drain the pasta well and transfer to a large bowl. While it is still piping hot, add the arugula mixture and toss gently until thoroughly combined. Transfer to a large, shallow serving bowl and arrange the tomato wedges around the edge. Serve immediately.

NOTE: The arugula mixture can be prepared up to 4 hours in advance. Just store it in a covered bowl in the refrigerator. Bring it back to room temperature before mixing it with the pasta.

Reminiscent of the sweet-and-spicy noodles found in Asian restaurants, this filling dish can be prepared at home in no time flat. Soba are Japanese noodles made from buckwheat. The optional cherry tomatoes add an unusual flavor twist and a welcome jolt of color.

Peanut Noodles

8 ounces soba or whole-grain spaghetti or fettuccine

3 tablespoons water

2 tablespoons smooth or chunky peanut butter

2 cloves garlic, minced

1 teaspoon reduced-sodium tamari

¼ teaspoon sea salt

¼ teaspoon chili powder

⅛ teaspoon cayenne

½ cucumber, peeled and julienned

12 cherry or grape tomatoes, halved (optional)

2 scallions, white and green parts, thinly sliced

Bring a large pot of salted water to a boil over medium-high heat. Stir in the soba. Decrease the heat to medium-low and cook, stirring occasionally, until tender but firm.

Meanwhile, put the water, peanut butter, garlic, tamari, salt, chili powder, and cayenne in a bowl large enough to also accommodate the soba. Whisk briskly until smooth.

Drain the soba well and pour it over the peanut butter mixture. Toss gently until thoroughly combined. To serve, spoon into deep bowls. Top each serving with some of the cucumber, optional tomatoes, and scallions. Serve warm, at room temperature, or thoroughly chilled.

NOTES

- You can cook the noodles up to 1 day in advance. Just store them in a covered bowl in the refrigerator. You can also use leftover cooked noodles, straight out of the refrigerator; aim for about 4 cups of cooked noodles.

- To prepare the dish in advance, or if you won't be serving all of it immediately, after stirring the noodles and peanut butter mixture together, cover and refrigerate. Serve chilled or at room temperature, topping with the cucumbers, optional tomatoes, and scallions just before serving.

This unique sauce bursts with sassy flavor. The tang from the green olives gives the pasta a real zing without overwhelming the dish. If you don't care for green olives, black olives also work well here.

Spicy Tomato and Green Olive Penne

1 can (28 ounces) whole tomatoes with juice, slightly mashed

20 green olives stuffed with pimientos, chopped

2 tablespoons chopped fresh basil, or 2 teaspoons dried

1 large clove garlic, minced, or ¼ teaspoon garlic powder

1 teaspoon brown sugar

1 teaspoon reduced-sodium tamari

⅛ teaspoon crushed red pepper flakes

⅛ teaspoon sea salt (optional)

12 ounces whole-grain penne or other pasta

Put the tomatoes, olives, basil, garlic, brown sugar, tamari, crushed red pepper flakes, and optional salt in a large, nonreactive skillet over medium heat. Stir until well combined. Decrease the heat to medium-low, partially cover to prevent splattering, and simmer, stirring occasionally, until quite thick, 20 to 25 minutes. If the sauce seems too thick, add water, 1 tablespoon at a time, to achieve the desired consistency. Cover and keep hot over low heat.

Meanwhile, bring a large pot of salted water to a boil over medium-high heat. Stir in the penne. Decrease the heat to medium-low, cover, and cook, stirring occasionally, until tender but firm. Drain the penne well, then add it to the skillet. Toss gently until thoroughly combined. Serve immediately.

I love the slightly bitter, slightly sweet taste of broccoli rabe. Here, it's combined with hearty garbanzo beans and garlic to make a simple dish that will wake up your taste buds. Crusty bread is an ideal accompaniment.

Penne with Garbanzo Beans and Broccoli Rabe

1 pound whole-grain penne or other pasta

2 tablespoons extra-virgin olive oil, plus more as needed

1 bunch broccoli rabe, trimmed and cut into 2- to 3-inch pieces

4 cloves garlic, chopped, or ½ teaspoon garlic powder

⅛ to ¼ teaspoon crushed red pepper flakes

1 can (15 ounces) garbanzo beans, drained and rinsed

Bring a large pot of salted water to a boil over medium-high heat. Stir in the penne. Decrease the heat to medium-low and cook, stirring occasionally, until tender but firm.

Meanwhile, heat the oil in a large skillet over medium heat. Add the broccoli rabe, garlic, and crushed red pepper flakes and stir to combine. Cover and cook over medium heat, stirring occasionally, until the broccoli rabe is slightly tender, about 5 minutes. Stir in the garbanzo beans. Decrease the heat to medium-low, cover, and simmer, stirring occasionally, until the broccoli rabe is tender and the beans are heated through, about 10 minutes, adding more oil or a bit of water as needed to prevent sticking.

Drain the penne well, then add it to the skillet. Toss gently until thoroughly combined. Serve immediately.

VARIATION: Substitute 1 can (15 ounces) of white beans for the garbanzo beans.

Because this dish makes use of store-bought marinara sauce, it's a good choice for busy weeknights, or whenever time is at a premium. To round it out while keeping things simple, the recipe also includes canned beans for heartiness, protein, and texture, and spinach for color and its fabulous nutritional profile.

Penne with White Beans and Baby Spinach

MAKES 2 TO 3 SERVINGS

4 ounces (4½ cups, lightly packed) **baby spinach**

1 can (15 ounces) **white beans, drained and rinsed**

2 cups **jarred marinara sauce**

1 teaspoon **brown sugar** (optional)

1 teaspoon **dried basil**

1 teaspoon **extra-virgin olive oil** (optional)

¼ teaspoon **crushed red pepper flakes**

8 ounces **whole wheat penne or other pasta**

Put the spinach, beans, marinara sauce, optional brown sugar, basil, optional oil, and crushed red pepper flakes in a large skillet over medium heat. Stir until well combined. Cook, stirring occasionally, until steaming hot but not boiling. Decrease the heat to medium-low, partially cover to prevent splattering, and simmer, stirring occasionally, for 15 to 20 minutes.

Meanwhile, bring a large pot of salted water to a boil over medium-high heat. Stir in the penne and cook, stirring occasionally, until tender but firm. Drain the penne well, then add it to the skillet. Toss gently until thoroughly combined. Serve immediately.

This pasta sauce has the hearty feel of a traditional meat sauce, but without the meat, of course. This is my go-to sauce when I want a quick, hearty topping for spaghetti or pasta. You can whip this together in no time using onions, vegan sausage, and some staple pantry items.

Snazzy Spaghetti

2 tablespoons extra-virgin olive oil

2 large onions, chopped

2 teaspoons dried basil

1 teaspoon reduced-sodium tamari

1 package (14 ounces) vegan ground sausage

1 jar (about 25 ounces) marinara sauce

4 cloves garlic, minced, or ½ teaspoon garlic powder

¼ teaspoon crushed red pepper flakes (optional)

1 pound whole-grain spaghetti or other pasta

Heat 1 tablespoon of the oil in a large skillet over medium heat. Add the onions and cook, stirring occasionally, until slightly softened, about 5 minutes. Stir in the basil, tamari, and remaining tablespoon of oil. Decrease the heat to medium-low, cover, and cook, stirring occasionally, until the onions are golden, about 15 minutes. Add the vegan sausage, breaking it up with a potato masher or large spoon. Cook, stirring occasionally, until the vegan sausage is slightly browned, about 5 minutes. Stir in the marinara sauce, garlic, and optional crushed red pepper flakes. Partially cover to prevent splattering and cook, stirring occasionally, for 20 to 30 minutes.

Meanwhile, bring a large pot of salted water to a boil. Add the spaghetti and cook, stirring occasionally, until tender but firm. Drain the spaghetti well, then add it to the skillet. Toss gently until thoroughly combined. Serve immediately.

Jazzy Tip Try using whole-grain lasagna noodles instead of traditional pasta. Break the lasagna noodles into large pieces, then cook them in boiling water until tender yet firm. Drain and toss with your favorite sauce. The lasagna noodles provide a homemade-noodle taste and texture to recipes without any extra fuss.

It's unusual for me to make a recipe with this many steps, but this dish is worth the effort. I based it on my grandma's traditional lasagna recipe and substituted tofu for the ricotta cheese and vegan ground round for the meat, then further lightened it up with long strips of zucchini in place of one of the layers of noodles. This lasagna freezes well, so the time you dedicate to making the dish will pay off in delicious leftovers later.

Festive Zucchini Lasagna

NOODLES

11 to 12 ounces whole-grain lasagna noodles

1 teaspoon extra-virgin olive oil

MUSHROOM SAUCE

3 tablespoons extra-virgin olive oil

8 ounces cremini or white button mushrooms, sliced

2 teaspoons reduced-sodium tamari

8 cloves garlic, minced

1 tablespoon italian seasoning

1 package (14 ounces) vegan ground round

2 heaping teaspoons brown sugar

1 jar (about 25 ounces) marinara sauce

1 can (28 ounces) crushed tomatoes

½ cup chopped fresh basil

To prepare the noodles, bring a large pot of salted water to a boil over medium-high heat. Add the noodles. Decrease the heat to medium-low and cook, stirring occasionally, until the noodles are almost tender. Drain and rinse under cool water, then drain well. Transfer to a large bowl. Drizzle with the oil and gently toss to coat.

Line a baking sheet with parchment paper. Spread some of the noodles on the lined baking sheet in a single layer. Top with another sheet of parchment paper and more noodles in a single layer. Continue in this way with the remaining noodles. (This will keep the noodles from sticking together while you prepare the rest of the recipe.)

To make the mushroom sauce, heat 2 tablespoons of the oil in a large skillet over medium heat. Add the mushrooms and cook, stirring occasionally, until slightly softened, about 4 minutes. Drizzle with the tamari and cook, stirring occasionally, for 2 minutes. Add the garlic and italian seasoning and cook, stirring occasionally, for 2 minutes. Add the vegan ground round, breaking it up with a potato masher or large spoon. Add a small amount of water, 1 tablespoon at a time, if the mixture seems dry. Stir in the brown sugar and cook, stirring frequently, until the vegan ground round is slightly browned, 2 to 3 minutes.

Stir the remaining tablespoon of oil into 1 cup of the marinara sauce and set aside. Stir the remaining marinara sauce, tomatoes, and basil into the mushroom mixture. Decrease the heat to low, partially cover to prevent splattering, and simmer, stirring occasionally, for 20 to 25 minutes.

TOFU RICOTTA

14 to 16 ounces firm regular tofu, drained

½ cup chopped fresh flat-leaf parsley

¼ teaspoon reduced-sodium tamari

Sea salt

Freshly ground pepper

ADDITIONAL INGREDIENTS

2 zucchini

12 to 15 ounces vegan
mozzarella cheese, shredded

3 tablespoons toasted wheat germ

5 ounces (5¾ cups, lightly packed)
baby spinach

1 teaspoon italian seasoning (optional)

Sea salt

Freshly ground pepper

Meanwhile, to make the tofu ricotta, put the tofu, parsley, and tamari in a medium bowl and mash with a potato masher until the mixture has the consistency of ricotta cheese. Season with salt and pepper to taste.

Preheat the oven to 400 degrees F.

Slice each zucchini lengthwise into ⅛- to ¼-inch thick strips.

Spread the reserved cup of marinara sauce evenly over the bottom of a 13 x 9-inch glass or ceramic baking pan. Arrange one-third of the lasagna noodles over the sauce. Spread one-third of the mushroom sauce over the noodles in an even layer. Top with all the zucchini, arranged lengthwise (in the same direction as the noodles), then all the tofu mixture, spread in

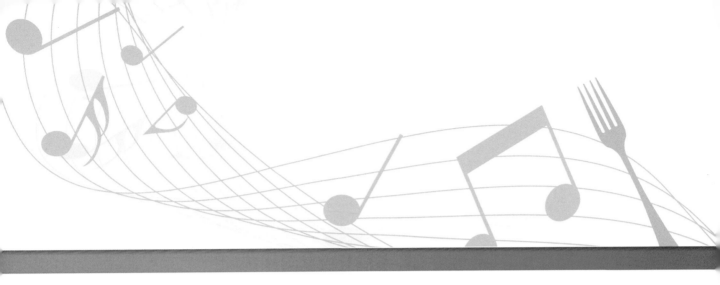

an even layer. Arrange another one-third of the noodles over the tofu mixture. Spread another one-third of the mushroom sauce over the noodles in an even layer. Scatter two-thirds of the vegan mozzarella over the mushroom sauce, then sprinkle with the toasted wheat germ. Top with all the spinach, pressing it down firmly. Arrange the remaining noodles over the spinach, then spread the remaining mushroom sauce over the noodles. Scatter the remaining vegan mozzarella over the top. Sprinkle the optional italian seasoning over the top, along with some salt and pepper if desired.

Cover and bake for about 55 minutes. Uncover and bake for 5 to 7 minutes, until slightly golden on top.

Let cool for 15 minutes. Serve warm.

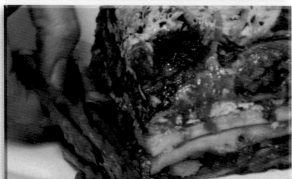

NOTE: You can cook the noodles up to 1 day in advance. Once they're cooked and spread out on a baking sheet between layers of parchment paper, wrap the baking sheet tightly in plastic wrap and refrigerate until you assemble the lasagna.

VARIATION: Substitute an additional 8 ounces of mushrooms, finely chopped, for the vegan ground round.

If you're in the mood for lasagna but not in the mood to spend over an hour putting it together, try this simplified version. Because no sautéing is required, these fancy rolls are ready for the oven in less than thirty minutes. To round out the meal, try Roasted Asparagus with Garlic and Tomatoes (page 165) and Grandma's Garlic Bread (page 171).

Quick Lasagna Rolls

8 whole-grain lasagna noodles

4½ teaspoons extra-virgin olive oil

1 jar (about 25 ounces) marinara sauce

14 to 16 ounces firm regular tofu, drained

1 cup chopped fresh basil

½ cup chopped fresh parsley

½ teaspoon reduced-sodium tamari

5 to 6 large green olives, preferably queen or sevillano, pitted and chopped (optional)

5 cloves garlic, chopped

2 tablespoons toasted wheat germ

2 cups shredded vegan cheese

Preheat the oven to 400 degrees F.

Bring a large pot of salted water to a boil over medium-high heat. Add the noodles. Decrease the heat to medium-low and cook, stirring occasionally, until the noodles are almost tender. Drain and rinse under cool water, then drain well. Transfer to a large bowl. Drizzle with 1 teaspoon of the oil and gently toss to coat. Allow the noodles to cool.

Meanwhile, stir 3 teaspoons of the oil into 1 cup of the marinara sauce. Spread the mixture in the bottom of an 11 x 7-inch glass or ceramic baking pan.

Put the tofu, ½ cup of the basil, and the parsley, tamari, and remaining ½ teaspoon of oil in a medium bowl and mash with a potato masher until the mixture has the consistency of ricotta cheese. Add the optional olives and the garlic and stir until thoroughly combined.

Lay a noodle on a large cutting board. Spoon about ¼ cup of the tofu mixture along the length of the noodle, spreading it evenly with the back of the spoon. Gently roll into a spiral shape. Set the roll in the baking pan seam-side down. Continue with the remaining noodles and filling, arranging them snugly in the pan.

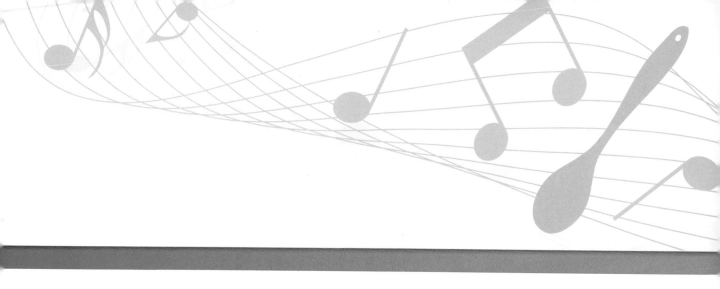

Set aside ¾ cup of the remaining marinara sauce. Spoon the remainder over the rolls, distributing it evenly. Sprinkle ¼ cup of the basil over the top.

Cover the pan with foil and bake for about 40 minutes. Remove the pan from the oven but do not turn the oven off. Spoon the remaining marinara sauce over the rolls, then sprinkle with the wheat germ, vegan cheese, and remaining ¼ cup of basil. Bake for about 15 minutes, until the sauce is bubbling and the top is slightly browned.

Put the pan on a wire rack. Let cool for 15 minutes. Serve 1 to 2 rolls per person, spooning the sauce from the bottom of the pan over top of the rolls.

This super-hearty casserole is my take on traditional baked ziti. It's interesting enough to bring to a potluck party, yet simple enough to make for a weeknight supper. A green salad is all you need to complete the meal.

Jazzy Baked Ziti

1 pound whole-grain ziti or other pasta

1 jar (about 25 ounces) marinara sauce

4 ounces (4½ cups, lightly packed) baby spinach

1 onion, chopped

3 stalks celery, with leaves, chopped

¼ cup red wine (optional)

1 tablespoon extra-virgin olive oil (optional)

1 teaspoon dried basil

½ teaspoon garlic powder

⅛ to ¼ teaspoon crushed red pepper flakes

⅓ cup toasted wheat germ

6 ounces shredded vegan cheese

Preheat the oven to 400 degrees F.

Bring a large pot of salted water to a boil over medium-high heat. Stir in the ziti. Decrease the heat to medium-low and cook, stirring occasionally, until the ziti is almost tender, 6 to 7 minutes. Drain well and transfer to a large bowl. Add the marinara sauce, spinach, onion, celery, optional wine, optional oil, basil, garlic powder, and crushed red pepper flakes. Toss gently until thoroughly combined.

Spread half of the ziti mixture in an even layer in a 13 x 9-inch glass or ceramic baking pan. Sprinkle the wheat germ evenly over it. Top with the remaining ziti mixture, spreading it in an even layer. Sprinkle the vegan cheese evenly over the top.

Cover the pan with foil and bake for 50 to 60 minutes, until bubbling, uncovering for the last 10 minutes to brown the top if desired. Serve immediately.

Marvelous
Main Dishes

Crispy Portobello Steaks, 128, Roasted Asparagus with Garlic and Tomatoes, 165, Maple Sweet Potatoes, 163

One of the food-related questions I'm asked most often is *"What can I substitute for meat,* especially when I'm preparing a meal for family or company?" There are so many options. First and foremost, I suggest *rethinking the question.* As the pasta recipes in chapter 8 abundantly indicate, a well-rounded plant-based dish can be *entirely satisfying* without any attempt to emulate or replace meat. One way to ensure that vegan meals satisfy the heartiest of appetites is to make main dishes featuring *robust veggies,* such as portobello mushrooms or winter squash. That said, meat analogs are a good option when transitioning from an omnivorous diet to plant-based eating. Adding crumbled veggie burgers, *vegan ground round,* or other meat analogs to pasta sauces, casseroles, and chili is the perfect way to get started. *Tofu and tempeh* can also stand in for meat. In addition to being excellent sources of complete protein, both offer a great canvas for highlighting the flavors of sauces and seasonings. The recipes in this chapter feature all of these approaches and range from dishes simple enough to prepare for weeknight suppers to festive entrées you'll be proud to serve at family get-togethers or formal dinner parties. Trust me: *no one will miss the meat.*

If you've never tried cooking tempeh before, this is a good recipe to start with. It's ready to pop in the oven in 10 minutes and has a wonderful sweet-and-savory flavor. The cooked tempeh is also great in sandwiches.

Maple-Mustard Baked Tempeh

MAKES 2 TO 3 SERVINGS

8 ounces tempeh

1 shallot, diced

2 heaping tablespoons dijon or spicy mustard

1 tablespoon extra-virgin olive oil

1 tablespoon maple syrup

Preheat the oven to 400 degrees F. Oil an 8-inch square baking pan.

Cut the tempeh in half lengthwise, then in half horizontally, to make 4 cutlets. Put the tempeh in the prepared pan in a single layer.

Put the shallot, mustard, oil, and maple syrup in a small bowl and stir until thoroughly combined. Spread the mixture evenly over the tempeh.

Cover with foil and bake for 20 to 30 minutes, until slightly browned and piping hot throughout. Serve immediately.

These tempeh cutlets are bathed in barbecue sauce and enhanced with onion and bell pepper. The combination of sweet onion and a lightly sweetened sauce flavors the tempeh to perfection.

Barbecue Tempeh Cutlets with Bell Pepper and Sweet Onion

8 ounces tempeh

1 cup barbecue sauce

2 teaspoons brown sugar

1 teaspoon extra-virgin olive oil

1 large sweet onion, thinly sliced

1 green bell pepper, chopped

Preheat the oven to 400 degrees F.

Cut the tempeh in half lengthwise, then in half horizontally, to make 4 cutlets. Put the barbecue sauce, brown sugar, and oil in a medium bowl and stir until thoroughly combined. Spread ⅓ cup of the mixture in the bottom of an 8-inch square baking pan. Put the tempeh in the pan in a single layer. Pour another ⅓ cup of the sauce mixture over the tempeh, spreading it evenly with a spatula.

Add the onion and bell pepper to the bowl with the remaining sauce mixture. Stir until the vegetables are evenly coated. Spread the mixture evenly over the tempeh.

Cover with foil and bake for 45 to 55 minutes, until the sauce is sizzling and the onion is soft. The tempeh may be served at this point or, to brown the onion a bit, uncover and bake for 8 to 12 minutes longer. Serve immediately.

NOTE: Serve the cutlets over rice, couscous, or quinoa, with a green vegetable on the side. Or, for a vegan take on a traditional barbecue meal, serve them on toasted whole-grain buns with Zesty Zucchini Oven Fries (page 163) or Fabulous Oven Fries (page 162) on the side.

In this recipe, a savory, crunchy coating perfectly complements the meaty texture and mouthwatering taste of portobello mushrooms. The method was inspired by my grandma's trick of using mayonnaise to keep chicken moist when baking. This dish is elegant enough for a formal dinner party,

Crispy Portobello Steaks

see photo, page 124   **MAKES 4 SERVINGS**

4 portobello mushrooms, stemmed

3 cups cornflakes

1 teaspoon italian seasoning

1 teaspoon garlic powder

¼ teaspoon sea salt

⅛ to ¼ teaspoon freshly ground pepper

2 to 3 tablespoons extra-virgin olive oil

⅓ cup vegan mayonnaise

2 teaspoons dijon mustard

2 teaspoons reduced-sodium tamari

Preheat the oven to 400 degrees F. Line a 13 x 9-inch baking pan with parchment paper.

Rinse the portobello mushrooms briefly and pat dry with a clean dish towel, taking care not to break them.

Put the cornflakes, italian seasoning, garlic powder, salt, and pepper in a blender or food processor and process to form crumbs. Transfer to a medium bowl. Add 1 tablespoon of the oil. Stir until the crumbs are evenly coated.

Put the vegan mayonnaise and mustard in a small bowl and whisk until thoroughly blended.

Lay a mushroom upside down on a large plate. Sprinkle ½ teaspoon of the tamari over the gills, then drizzle with 1 teaspoon of the oil. Turn the mushroom over and spread one-quarter of the mayonnaise mixture evenly over the top. Spread one-quarter of the cornflake mixture evenly over the top, patting it down firmly and not leaving any holes or gaps. Put the mushroom in the lined pan, right-side up. Repeat with the remaining ingredients.

Tent the baking pan with foil and bake for 20 minutes. Turn the heat down to 375 degrees F, remove the foil, and bake for 10 to 20 minutes, until the mushrooms are fork-tender and the coating is crispy.

Let cool for 5 to 10 minutes to firm up. Cut the mushrooms into thick diagonal slices and serve immediately.

especially when paired with Maple Sweet Potatoes (page 163) and Roasted Asparagus with Garlic and Tomatoes (page 165). Or, for a satisfying weeknight supper, try serving the mushrooms nestled atop mashed potatoes or cooked quinoa or rice, with any green vegetable on the side.

This delectable loaf is crisp on the outside, tender on the inside, and bursting with flavor. Paired with Mashed Potatoes and Cauliflower (page 158) and Sesame Greens Beans (page 150), it makes for a traditional American-style meal that even meat lovers will enjoy.

Wonderful Walnut-Mushroom Loaf

2 to 3 tablespoons extra-virgin olive oil, as needed

1 large bermuda onion, chopped

8 to 10 ounces cremini or white button mushrooms, chopped

2 cloves garlic, minced

1 heaping teaspoon brown sugar

1 teaspoon reduced-sodium tamari

2¼ cups walnuts

½ cup unsalted roasted sunflower seeds

2½ cups fresh whole-grain breadcrumbs

1 cup shredded vegan cheese

Zest from ½ lemon

1 teaspoon italian seasoning

¼ teaspoon sea salt

2 cups jarred marinara sauce

Preheat the oven to 400 degrees F.

Heat 2 tablespoons of the oil in a large skillet over medium heat. Add the onion and cook, stirring occasionally, until the onion is translucent, 8 to 10 minutes. Add 5 to 6 ounces of the chopped mushrooms and cook, stirring occasionally, for 2 to 3 minutes. Stir in the garlic, brown sugar, and tamari. Decrease the heat to medium-low, cover, and cook, stirring occasionally, until the mushrooms are golden around the edges and the pan juices have evaporated, 5 to 10 minutes, adding more oil or a bit of water as needed to prevent sticking.

Meanwhile, put the walnuts in a food processor and process until coarsely ground. Transfer to a large bowl. Put the sunflower seeds in the

food processor and process until coarsely ground. Add the sunflower seeds to the walnuts, along with the onion mixture, breadcrumbs, vegan cheese, zest, italian seasoning, and salt. Stir until thoroughly combined.

Stir 1 teaspoon of the remaining oil into 1 cup of the marinara sauce. Spread the mixture in the bottom of a 13 x 9-inch glass or ceramic baking pan. Working with one-third of the mushroom mixture at a time, mold it by hand into a large ball, compressing it to release the oils in the walnuts and help hold the loaf together. Put the balls in the baking pan side by side and form them into a single compact loaf, patting it down and smoothing the top.

Scatter the remaining mushrooms around the loaf. Spoon ⅔ cup of the remaining marinara sauce over the mushrooms. Spoon the remaining ⅓ cup of marinara sauce over the top of the loaf, spreading it evenly with a rubber spatula.

Cover with foil and bake for 40 to 45 minutes. Remove the foil and bake for 10 to 15 minutes, until the loaf is almost firm to the touch.

Let cool for 10 to 15 minutes to firm up. Cut the loaf into generous slices. Serve warm, with some of the mushrooms and sauce from the pan spooned over each serving. Put the remaining mushrooms and sauce in a gravy boat or small bowl to pass at the table.

A great choice for a cold winter's night, this filling stew is even more substantial when served over pasta, rice, millet, or quinoa. If you don't have all of the veggies listed, just substitute whatever you have on hand and adjust the cooking time accordingly. Note that all of the vegetables are ultimately steamed together, so you'll need an extra-large steamer.

Steamed Vegetable Stew

MAKES 4 SERVINGS

2 medium white potatoes, peeled and cubed

2 medium sweet potatoes, peeled and cubed

5 to 6 carrots, sliced

1 parsnip, sliced

2 to 3 cloves garlic, chopped

1 small onion, chopped

1 cup cut green beans, in 1- to 2-inch pieces

8 to 10 cremini or white button mushrooms, sliced

2 stalks celery, with leaves, sliced

4 to 8 ounces spinach, stemmed and coarsely chopped

1½ cups vegetable broth

1 tablespoon whole-grain flour

1 teaspoon dried basil, italian seasoning, or other dried herb blend

1 teaspoon reduced-sodium tamari

⅛ to ¼ teaspoon ground cinnamon (optional)

Freshly ground pepper

Steam the white potatoes, sweet potatoes, carrots, parsnip, and garlic for 15 minutes. Add the onion, green beans, mushrooms, and celery and steam for 10 minutes. Add the spinach and steam just until the root vegetables are fork-tender and the spinach wilts, about 5 minutes.

Meanwhile, put the broth, flour, basil, tamari, and optional cinnamon in a blender and process until smooth. Transfer to a soup pot over medium-low heat and cook, stirring often, until steaming hot but not boiling. Add the steamed vegetables and stir gently until well combined. Cook, stirring occasionally, until the liquid thickens and the vegetables are heated through, 5 to 7 minutes. Serve piping hot.

Jazzy Tip Okay, I'll admit it. I sometimes use presliced mushrooms when I'm in a rush, especially for making well-cooked dishes, such as sauces, casseroles, or soups. Just rinse the sliced mushrooms thoroughly before using them.

This riff on rice and beans is high on taste but low on effort. If you don't have all the spices listed below, no worries; just omit them or substitute other seasonings. This is a forgiving recipe that works well in endless variations, so feel free to experiment.

Easy Rice and Beans

MAKES 3 TO 4 SERVINGS

1 tablespoon extra-virgin olive oil

1 onion, chopped

4 cloves garlic, chopped

1 teaspoon dried cilantro

1 teaspoon reduced-sodium tamari

½ teaspoon ground cumin

½ teaspoon ground turmeric

Pinch crushed red pepper flakes

2¼ cups vegetable broth

1 can (15 ounces) black beans, drained and rinsed

1 cup brown basmati rice or short-grain brown rice, rinsed

Heat the oil in a large saucepan over medium heat. Add the onion, garlic, cilantro, tamari, cumin, turmeric, and crushed red pepper flakes and cook, stirring occasionally, until the onion is soft, about 8 minutes. Stir in the broth, beans, and rice and bring to a boil. Decrease the heat to medium-low, cover, and simmer for 45 to 50 minutes, until the rice is soft but not mushy. Fluff and serve.

A hint of cinnamon adds a sweet undertone that jazzes up this cold-weather favorite. The chili is satisfying on its own, or, for heartier appetites, try spooning it over fluffy baked potatoes.

Cinnamon-Spiced Three-Bean Chili

pictured on back cover **MAKES 8 SERVINGS**

1 large bermuda onion, chopped

¾ cup vegetable broth, plus more as needed

1 small bunch celery, with leaves, chopped

1 tablespoon chopped fresh cilantro, or 1 teaspoon dried

1 to 2 teaspoons reduced-sodium tamari

1 teaspoon chili powder

¼ to ½ teaspoon ground cinnamon

⅛ teaspoon cayenne

1 package (14 ounces) **vegan ground sausage** (see variation)

1 jar (about 25 ounces) **marinara sauce**

1 can (15 ounces) **kidney beans, drained and rinsed**

1 can (15 ounces) **black beans, drained and rinsed**

1 can (15 ounces) **white beans, drained and rinsed**

1 can (15 ounces) **corn, drained**

3 cloves garlic, chopped

Put the onion and 2 tablespoons of the broth in a soup pot over medium heat. Cook, stirring occasionally, until the onion is slightly softened, about 5 minutes. Stir in the celery, cilantro, 1 teaspoon of the tamari, ½ teaspoon of the chili powder, ¼ teaspoon of the cinnamon, a pinch of the cayenne, and 2 more tablespoons of broth. Cook, stirring occasionally, until the celery is tender, about 5 minutes.

Add the vegan sausage, breaking it up with a potato masher or large spoon. Cook, stirring occasionally, for 5 minutes, adding more broth, 1 tablespoon at a time, as needed to prevent sticking. Stir in the marinara sauce, beans, corn, garlic, the remaining ½ cup of broth and ½ teaspoon of chili powder, and another pinch of cayenne. Taste and add the remaining teaspoon of tamari and ¼ teaspoon of cinnamon if desired.

Decrease the heat to medium-low, cover, and simmer, stirring often, for 1 hour, adding more broth as needed to achieve the desired consistency. Serve piping hot.

VARIATION: Substitute an additional can of beans, any variety, for the vegan sausage.

Jazzy Tip: I live in the Northeast, and fresh local tomatoes are only available a few months out of the year. For this reason, store-bought low-fat marinara sauce and salsa are both star staples in my pantry. Find several varieties that you enjoy and keep them on hand for when good-quality tomatoes aren't available or you need to put together a meal in a hurry.

This hearty chili is easy to whip up, and ever so welcome on a brisk winter afternoon. While it's a great one-pot weeknight supper, it's also special enough to offer as an enticing entrée when company is coming for dinner. Serve it with a crisp green salad, Double-Corn Cornbread (page 57), and, to round out the perfect fireside menu, Sweet-and-Spicy Chocolate Mousse (page 175) for dessert.

Jazzy Black Bean Chili

MAKES 3 TO 4 SERVINGS

1 tablespoon extra-virgin olive oil, plus more as needed

1 large sweet onion, chopped

2 stalks celery, with leaves, chopped

2 teaspoons chili powder

1 to 2 teaspoons dried cilantro

1 teaspoon reduced-sodium tamari

⅛ teaspoon cayenne (optional)

10 ounces vegan ground round

2 cloves garlic, chopped

1 can (15 ounces) black beans, drained and rinsed

1 can (15 ounces) corn, drained

1 can (15 ounces) crushed tomatoes

2 small zucchini, diced

⅛ teaspoon sea salt

Vegan sour cream, for serving (optional)

Heat the oil in a soup pot over medium heat. Add the onion and cook, stirring occasionally, until slightly softened, about 5 minutes. Add the celery and cook, stirring occasionally, until the celery is tender, about 5 minutes. Stir in 1 teaspoon of the chili powder, 1 teaspoon of the cilantro, and the tamari and optional cayenne. Cook, stirring often, until the onion is golden, about 10 minutes.

Add the vegan ground round, breaking it up with a potato masher or large spoon. Cook, stirring occasionally, until the vegan ground round is slightly browned, about 5 minutes, adding more oil or a bit of water as needed to prevent sticking. Add the garlic and cook, stirring constantly, for 1 minute. Stir in the beans, corn, tomatoes, zucchini, salt, and remaining teaspoon of chili powder. Taste and add the remaining teaspoon of cilantro if desired.

Decrease the heat to medium-low, cover, and simmer, stirring occasionally, for 45 to 60 minutes. Serve piping hot, topped with vegan sour cream and a sprinkling of cilantro if desired.

NOTE: If a stronger cilantro taste is desired, use 2 to 4 tablespoons of chopped fresh cilantro in place of the dried cilantro.

Easy to prepare and oh so tasty, this hearty entrée makes a wonderful one-dish meal for those evenings when time is at a premium. This is one of the first vegetarian recipes I developed, and it's great to serve to people new to a vegan diet.

Black Bean Burritos

MAKES 2 TO 4 SERVINGS

1 jar (16 ounces) salsa, as needed

4 whole-grain flour tortillas

1 can (15 ounces) black beans, drained and rinsed

1½ cups shredded vegan cheese

5 to 6 cups mixed baby greens or thinly sliced romaine lettuce

2 tomatoes, chopped

Preheat the oven to 400 degrees F. Lightly oil a 13 x 9-inch glass or ceramic baking pan.

Spread a thin layer of salsa over the bottom of the prepared pan. Lay a tortilla on a flat surface. Arrange one-quarter of the beans evenly over the lower half of the tortilla. Top the beans with 2 tablespoons of the salsa and ¼ cup of the vegan cheese.

Starting at the bottom edge, roll the tortilla tightly and evenly around the filling. Set the burrito seam-side down in the prepared pan. Repeat to make the remaining burritos. Scatter the remaining ½ cup of vegan cheese over the burritos.

Cover with foil and bake for 20 to 25 minutes, until the vegan cheese is melted and the burritos are heated through, uncovering for the last 3 to 4 minutes of baking to crisp the tortillas if desired. Serve hot, topping each burrito with one-quarter of the mixed baby greens and tomatoes and more salsa as desired.

VARIATION: Substitute pinto or kidney beans for the black beans.

I like to serve this delectable squash as an enticing entrée throughout the winter holiday season. Use the stuffing recipe suggested below if you like, or showcase familiar flavors with whatever stuffing your family and friends are accustomed to.

Stuffed Acorn Squash

2 small acorn squash, halved and seeded

1 teaspoon extra-virgin olive oil

Sea salt

Freshly ground pepper

4 cups Mushroom, Walnut, and Celery Stuffing (page 169), **prepared and ready to bake**

4 tablespoons shredded vegan cheese (optional)

Preheat the oven to 400 degrees F. Lightly oil a 13 x 9-inch baking pan.

Put the squash halves cut-side up in the prepared pan. Brush ¼ teaspoon of the oil over the upper surface of each squash half. Sprinkle with salt and pepper. Spoon 1 cup of the stuffing into each squash half.

Cover the pan with foil and bake for 30 to 40 minutes, until the squash is fork-tender. Sprinkle 1 tablespoon of the optional vegan cheese over each squash half and bake, uncovered, for 10 to 15 minutes, until the stuffing is brown and crispy and the vegan cheese is melted. Serve immediately.

These stuffed artichokes are simply stunning—and fun to eat. The savory filling melds wonderfully with the slightly sweet taste of the artichokes. For a delightful meal, serve the artichokes with a bountiful green salad. Be sure to provide empty bowls at the table for discarding the inedible part of the artichoke leaves.

Baked Artichokes with Savory Walnut Stuffing

MAKES 4 SERVINGS

ARTICHOKES

½ onion, coarsely chopped

1 tablespoon balsamic, cider, or red wine vinegar

4 large artichokes, trimmed (see note, page 63)

STUFFING

4 slices sprouted whole-grain bread or other whole-grain bread, torn or cut into small pieces

1 cup chopped walnuts

8 large cremini or white button mushrooms, diced

1 sweet onion, finely chopped

¾ to 1 cup shredded vegan cheese (optional)

3 tablespoons extra-virgin olive oil

2 cloves garlic, minced

1 teaspoon italian seasoning

½ teaspoon garlic powder

Sea salt

Freshly ground pepper

ADDITIONAL INGREDIENTS

Extra-virgin olive oil, for drizzling

Lemon Dipping Sauce (see page 156), for serving

To prepare the artichokes, put 2 to 4 inches of water in a deep saucepan large enough to hold all the artichokes snugly so they remain upright as they cook. Add the onion and vinegar. Put the artichokes in the pan and bring to a boil over medium-high heat. Decrease the heat to medium, cover, and cook until barely tender, 20 to 25 minutes, rotating the artichokes halfway through the cooking time. Let cool slightly.

Preheat the oven to 350 degrees F. Line a 13 x 9-inch baking pan with parchment paper.

While the artichokes are cooking, prepare the stuffing. Put the bread, walnuts, mushrooms, onion, optional vegan cheese, oil, garlic, italian seasoning, and garlic powder in a large bowl and stir until thoroughly combined. Season with salt and pepper.

When the artichokes are cool enough to handle, carefully pull the outer leaves back and pull out and discard the small, spiky inner leaves. Scoop out the fuzzy center choke with a teaspoon. Fill the cavity of each artichoke with some of the stuffing. Spread the larger leaves apart and spoon more stuffing between them, dividing the remaining stuffing equally among the artichokes.

Put the artichokes in the lined pan and drizzle with a bit of oil. Tent loosely with foil and bake for 50 to 55 minutes, until the artichokes are soft and the stuffing is brown and crispy around the edges. Serve warm, at room temperature, or chilled, with the dipping sauce alongside in small bowls.

Brimming with savory stuffing, these artichokes make a delectable first course or light entrée. Purchase large, firm artichokes for this dish so they'll hold together while baking. Be sure to provide empty bowls at the table for discarding the inedible part of the artichoke leaves.

Italian-Style Stuffed Artichokes

2 large artichokes, trimmed (see note, page 63)

2 teaspoons extra-virgin olive oil

1 cup jarred marinara sauce

1 slice sprouted whole-grain bread or other whole-grain bread, coarsely torn

½ cup unsalted roasted sunflower seeds

½ cup chopped walnuts

½ teaspoon italian seasoning

½ cup shredded vegan cheese

5 large green olives, preferably queen or sevillano, pitted and chopped

Put 2 to 4 inches of water in a deep saucepan large enough to hold the artichokes snugly so they remain upright as they cook. Put the artichokes in the pan and bring to a boil over medium-high heat. Decrease the heat to medium, cover, and cook until barely tender, 20 to 25 minutes, rotating the artichokes halfway through the cooking time. Let cool slightly.

Preheat the oven to 400 degrees F.

While the artichokes are cooking, stir 1 teaspoon of the oil into ¾ cup of the marinara sauce. Spread the mixture in the bottom of a 13 x 9-inch glass or ceramic baking pan.

Put the bread, sunflower seeds, walnuts, and italian seasoning in a food processor and process into coarse crumbs. Transfer to a medium bowl. Add the vegan cheese, remaining teaspoon of oil, and olives and stir until thoroughly combined.

When the artichokes are cool enough to handle, cut them in half vertically. Scoop out the fuzzy center choke with a teaspoon. Put the artichokes in the baking pan cut-side up. Stuff each cavity with one-quarter of the sunflower seed mixture, mounding it if need be. Spoon 1 tablespoon of the remaining marinara sauce over each artichoke.

Cover with foil and bake for 40 to 50 minutes. Uncover and bake for 10 minutes to brown the top of the stuffing. Put the sauce from the pan in a gravy boat or small bowl to pass at the table. Serve immediately.

This is an excellent dish to serve to people new to vegan fare—it's elegant enough for company and special enough for a romantic dinner for two. The texture and flavor replicate a traditional stroganoff.

Mushroom-Tempeh Stroganoff

1 tablespoon extra-virgin olive oil

1 bermuda onion, chopped

8 ounces cremini or white button mushrooms, sliced

1 teaspoon dried basil

1 teaspoon reduced-sodium tamari

Pinch cayenne

2 to 3 cups vegetable broth, plus more as needed

8 ounces tempeh, cut into quarters and thinly sliced

1 tablespoon whole wheat flour or oat flour

Sea salt

Freshly ground pepper

8 ounces whole-grain noodles, cooked and drained, or 1½ cups cooked brown rice, kept hot

Chopped fresh parsley, for garnish

Heat the oil in a large skillet over medium heat. Add the onion and cook, stirring occasionally, until slightly softened, about 5 minutes. Add the mushrooms, basil, ½ teaspoon of the tamari, and the cayenne and cook, stirring occasionally, until the mushrooms are tender, about 8 minutes, adding a bit of broth as needed to prevent sticking. Add the tempeh and cook, stirring occasionally, until browned, about 8 minutes. Stir in 1 cup of the broth. Decrease the heat to medium-low, partially cover, and simmer, stirring occasionally, for 15 to 20 minutes, adding more broth as needed to keep the mixture very moist.

Put the flour in a small cup or bowl, whisk in ½ cup of the broth, and stir into the mushroom mixture. Cook, stirring constantly, until the liquid has thickened to form a gravy. Season with the remaining ½ teaspoon of tamari and salt and pepper to taste. If the gravy is too thick, thin with additional broth to achieve the desired consistency. Serve immediately over the noodles, garnished with parsley if desired.

VARIATION: Replace the tempeh with an additional 8 ounces of mushrooms.

This tempting, hearty entrée is especially well-suited to wintertime, and the festive presentation will grace the table at any holiday celebration. Choose the color of peppers accordingly: orange and yellow for Thanksgiving, red and green for Christmas, or red for Valentine's Day. The quinoa has a

Fancy Stuffed Peppers with Quinoa and Black Beans

1 cup quinoa, rinsed thoroughly

2 cups vegetable broth

6 bell peppers, any color or a combination of colors

1 tablespoon extra-virgin olive oil

1 jar (about 25 ounces) marinara sauce, as needed

1 can (15 ounces) black beans, drained and rinsed

6 ounces cremini or white button mushrooms, chopped

1 onion, chopped

¼ cup toasted wheat germ, plus more as needed

2 cloves garlic, chopped

1 teaspoon dried basil

Put the quinoa and broth in a medium saucepan and bring to a boil over medium-high heat. Decrease the heat to medium-low, cover, and simmer for about 15 minutes, until the water is absorbed and the quinoa is soft but not mushy. Let cool slightly. Transfer to a bowl, cover, and refrigerate for 2 to 24 hours.

When ready to assemble the stuffed peppers, preheat the oven to 400 degrees F.

Slice off the top ½ to ¾ inches of each pepper and set aside (these tops will be used to "cap" the peppers later). Seed the peppers.

Stir the oil into ½ cup of the marinara sauce. Spread the mixture in the bottom of a deep casserole large enough to hold all the peppers snugly so they remain upright during baking.

Set aside ¼ cup of the remaining marinara sauce. Mix the quinoa with the beans, mushrooms, onion, wheat germ, garlic, basil, and half of the remaining marinara sauce. Stir until well combined, adding more marinara sauce, a couple of tablespoonfuls at a time, until the mixture is moist but not soupy. If the mixture does get a little soupy, simply add more wheat germ.

Spoon one-quarter of the mixture into each pepper, mounding it if need be. Spoon 1 tablespoon of the reserved marinara sauce over each pepper, light, nutty flavor that perfectly complements the texture and bold taste of the black beans. As a bonus, any leftovers will be tasty even if served cold. One heads-up: It's best to make the quinoa a day in advance to allow it to firm up, so plan ahead.

Fancy Stuffed Peppers with Sweet-and-Savory Kale, 151

then top with the pepper tops. (The stuffing will peek out between the pepper tops and bottoms.) Carefully position the peppers in the casserole so they will remain upright while baking.

Cover and bake for 45 to 60 minutes, until the sauce is bubbly and the peppers are slightly tender but not mushy. Serve immediately or let cool for 15 minutes before serving. Put the sauce that has accumulated at the bottom of the casserole in a gravy boat or small bowl to pass at the table.

I like to serve these fancy fungi as an entrée at dinner parties, especially during the winter holidays. The meaty taste and texture of the portobellos is beautifully complemented by the steamy stuffing and crisp topping. For a showstopping meal, serve with Yam Casserole (page 164) or Maple Sweet Potatoes (page 163) and Nino's Broccoli Rabe with Garlic (page 153) or Sweet-and-Savory Kale (page 151).

Perfect Party Portobellos

4 slices sprouted whole-grain or other whole-grain bread, coarsely torn

2 teaspoons italian seasoning

2¾ cups walnuts

3 to 4 tablespoons extra-virgin olive oil

1 large sweet onion, chopped

3 to 4 stalks celery, with leaves, chopped

2 ounces cremini or white button mushrooms, chopped

1½ teaspoons reduced-sodium tamari, plus more as needed

1 heaping teaspoon brown sugar (optional)

1 cup shredded vegan cheese

¼ cup toasted wheat germ

3 cloves garlic, chopped

10 portobello mushrooms, stemmed

¼ cup chopped fresh parsley

¼ teaspoon sea salt

Preheat the oven to 400 degrees F. Line two large, rimmed baking sheets with parchment paper.

Put the bread and 1 teaspoon of the italian seasoning in a food processor and process into crumbs. Transfer to a large bowl. Put the walnuts in the food processor and process until coarsely ground. Put ¾ cup of the ground walnuts in a small bowl and set aside. Add the remaining walnuts to the bowl with the breadcrumbs.

Heat 1 tablespoon of the oil in a large skillet over medium heat. Add the onion, celery, and cremini mushrooms and cook, stirring occasionally, until the vegetables are tender, 10 to 15 minutes. Stir in 1 teaspoon of the tamari, the optional brown sugar, and the remaining teaspoon of italian seasoning. Decrease the heat to medium-low, cover, and cook, stirring occasionally, until the vegetables are slightly browned, about 10 minutes. Transfer to the bowl with the breadcrumbs. Add the vegan cheese, wheat germ, garlic, and 1 tablespoon of the oil and stir until thoroughly combined. If the breadcrumb mixture isn't moist enough to hold together, add more oil, 1 teaspoon at a time.

Rinse the portobello mushrooms briefly and pat dry with a clean dish towel, taking care not to break them.

Using the same skillet, pour in about ½ inch of water. Stir in the remaining ½ teaspoon of tamari. Put as many portobellos in the skillet as will fit in a single layer, placing them upside down. Cook just until the underside is slightly softened, about 3 minutes. Turn and cook the other side for 1 minute. Transfer to the lined baking sheets, placing the mushrooms upside down. Repeat with the remaining portobellos, adding more water and tamari as needed to keep the depth of liquid to about ½ inch.

Divide the breadcrumb mixture evenly among the portobellos, mounding about ⅓ cup of the mixture in each (an ice-cream scoop works well). Press the mixture firmly in place so it will adhere to the mushroom while baking.

Put the reserved ¾ cup of walnuts and the parsley, salt, and 1 teaspoon of oil in a small bowl and toss until thoroughly combined. Scatter the mixture evenly over the mushrooms, using about 1½ tablespoons per mushroom and patting it firmly in place.

Tent the mushrooms with foil and bake for 30 minutes. Remove the foil and, if desired, brush or drizzle a bit of oil (about 1 tablespoon in all) over the top of the mushrooms. Bake for 15 to 30 minutes longer, until the topping is crisp and the mushrooms are tender. Serve immediately.

Vegetable Delights and Sides

Basil Roasted Peppers, 160

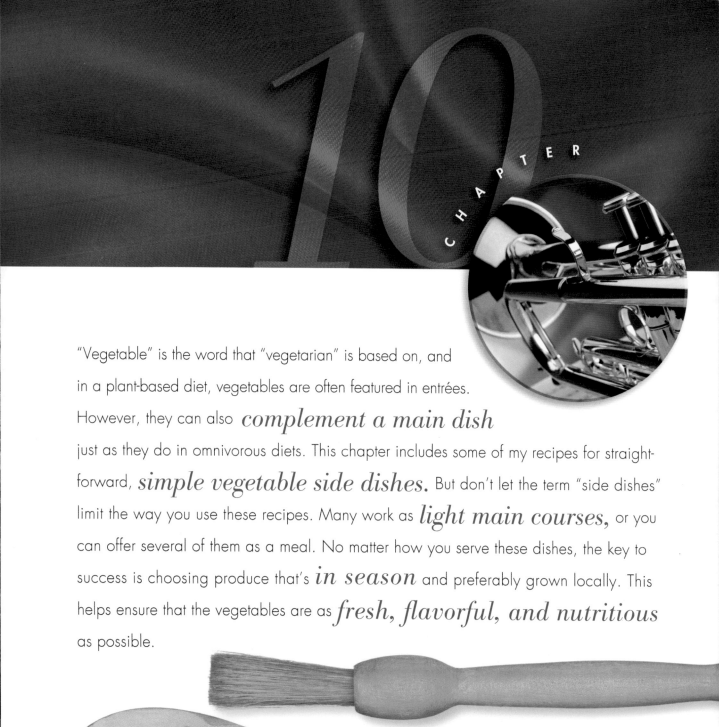

CHAPTER 10

"Vegetable" is the word that "vegetarian" is based on, and in a plant-based diet, vegetables are often featured in entrées. However, they can also *complement a main dish* just as they do in omnivorous diets. This chapter includes some of my recipes for straightforward, *simple vegetable side dishes.* But don't let the term "side dishes" limit the way you use these recipes. Many work as *light main courses,* or you can offer several of them as a meal. No matter how you serve these dishes, the key to success is choosing produce that's *in season* and preferably grown locally. This helps ensure that the vegetables are as *fresh, flavorful, and nutritious* as possible.

This raw side dish is low in calories, a breeze to prepare, and fabulous fare on a hot summer night. The zucchini strips really do look and taste a lot like fresh pasta.

Zucchini Fettuccine with Fresh Tomato Salsa

MAKES 4 SERVINGS

2 medium to large zucchini

2 ripe tomatoes, chopped

10 to 14 leaves fresh basil, minced

1 tablespoon extra-virgin olive oil

2 cloves garlic, minced

⅛ to ¼ teaspoon sea salt

Freshly ground pepper

Shave the zucchini lengthwise with a vegetable peeler to make the "noodles." Put the zucchini in a large bowl. Add the tomatoes, basil, oil, and garlic and toss gently until thoroughly combined. Season with salt and pepper to taste. Serve immediately.

When green beans are in season at my local farmers' market, I like to feature them as a simple side dish, accented with gomasio, which adds unusual dimensions of texture and flavor to the beans. But if you don't have any on hand, you can substitute sesame seeds. Because gomasio contains salt, seasoning with salt is optional here, and you should definitely taste before adding it.

Sesame Green Beans

MAKES 4 TO 5 SERVINGS

1 pound green beans, trimmed

2 teaspoons vegan margarine

1 to 2 teaspoons gomasio (see note) or sesame seeds

Sea salt (optional)

Freshly ground pepper

Steam the green beans until crisp-tender, 7 to 10 minutes. Transfer to a medium bowl and add the margarine. Season with the gomasio to taste. Toss gently until the green beans are evenly coated. Season with salt and pepper to taste. Serve immediately.

NOTE: Gomasio is a condiment made from ground roasted sesame seeds and salt, and sometimes sea vegetables or other ingredients. For an additional flavor note, try seaweed gomasio in this dish.

In this appealing side dish, brown sugar adds the sweet, while the tamari provides the savory. It is a beautiful dish that will enhance any meal—and a great introduction to cooking kale, as it takes the mystery out of preparing this fantastically nutritious leafy green vegetable.

Sweet-and-Savory Kale

see photo, page 143   **MAKES 4 TO 6 SERVINGS**

1 large bunch kale, stemmed, washed (see tip), **and very thinly sliced**

2 tablespoons extra-virgin olive oil

2 teaspoons brown sugar

2 teaspoons reduced-sodium tamari

4 teaspoons unsalted roasted sunflower seeds

Steam the kale until wilted and quite soft but still bright green, 15 to 20 minutes. Transfer to a medium bowl. Put the oil, brown sugar, and tamari in a small bowl and whisk to combine. Pour the mixture over the kale and toss until the kale is evenly coated. Sprinkle the sunflower seeds over the kale and toss lightly. Serve immediately.

NOTE: For a lower-calorie dish, use only 1 tablespoon of olive oil and increase the amount of tamari to taste.

Jazzy Tip Thoroughly cleaning dark leafy greens—such as kale, spinach, dandelion greens, and collard greens—is essential, as they often have sandy residue, especially along the stems and in crevices. Here is a foolproof method for cleaning greens to ensure they won't be gritty:

1. Put the greens in a very large bowl, then put the bowl in the sink.

2. Cover the greens with cold water and let them soak for a minute or two.

3. Swish the greens around gently so you don't bruise their delicate leaves.

4. Scoop them out of the bowl and put them in a large colander (also in the sink) to drain.

5. Empty the bowl and rinse it well.

6. Repeat until there is no sand or dirt in the bowl after you remove the greens.

7. If you are using the greens raw, such as in a salad or sandwich, it's important to dry them thoroughly. A salad spinner is perfect for the job, or you can carefully pat the leaves dry with a clean towel. If you will be cooking the greens, there's no need to dry them thoroughly. The droplets that remain on the leaves after rinsing will help the greens stay moist while cooking.

Although leeks are related to onions, they have a beautiful pale green color and subtle flavor that produce an attractive, delicate-tasting side dish.

Lovely Leeks

1 tablespoon extra-virgin olive oil

4 to 5 large leeks, white and light green parts, cleaned (see note) and thinly sliced

Sea salt

Freshly ground pepper

Heat the oil in a large skillet over medium heat. Add the leeks, cover, and cook, stirring occasionally, until they begin to soften, 3 to 5 minutes. Season with salt and pepper. Continue to cook, stirring occasionally, until slightly transparent and soft but not mushy, 2 to 3 minutes. Serve immediately.

NOTE: Leeks must be cleaned thoroughly to remove the fine sand and dirt often embedded between the layers. Here's a quick and easy way to do the job: Split the leeks lengthwise. Put them in a large bowl filled with cold water and soak briefly to loosen any debris. Then rinse thoroughly under cold water, parting the layers slightly so the debris rinses away. Put the leeks in a clean bowl of cold water and swish to remove any remaining sand or dirt.

My friend Nino, who hails from Puglia, taught me how to make this authentic Italian dish. The slightly bitter yet sweet taste of broccoli rabe makes this dish a great accompaniment to Quick Lasagna Rolls (page 120), Crispy Portobello Steaks (page 128), or Wonderful Walnut-Mushroom Loaf (page 130).

Nino's Broccoli Rabe with Garlic

MAKES 4 SERVINGS

2 tablespoons extra-virgin olive oil, plus more as needed

1 bunch broccoli rabe, trimmed and cut into bite-sized pieces

3 cloves garlic, chopped

¼ teaspoon crushed red pepper flakes

1 teaspoon reduced-sodium tamari (optional)

Sea salt (optional)

Put 1 tablespoon of the oil in a large skillet, then spread half of the broccoli rabe over it. Scatter the garlic over the broccoli rabe, then drizzle with half the remaining oil and sprinkle with the crushed red pepper flakes. Add a final layer of the remaining broccoli rabe and drizzle with the remaining oil. Press the broccoli rabe firmly into the skillet with the lid. Cook over medium-low heat for 8 to 10 minutes, stirring often and adding more oil or a bit of water as needed to prevent sticking. Season with the optional tamari, salt to taste, or both and cook, stirring frequently, for 3 to 5 minutes, until crisp-tender and still bright green. Serve immediately.

NOTE

- To turn this dish into a simple but delicious entrée, simply toss it with piping hot pasta.
- When purchasing broccoli rabe, make sure the florets and leaves are green, with no yellowing edges, and the stems are firm, not mushy.

These sweet-and-tangy artichokes make a sensational first course when you're having company over. The artichokes can be cooked up to a day in advance, allowing you to finish making the dish in a mere ten minutes.

Caramelized Balsamic Artichokes

MAKES 2 TO 4 SERVINGS

ARTICHOKES

2 artichokes, trimmed (see note, page 63)

2 tablespoons extra-virgin olive oil, plus more as needed

2 teaspoons reduced-sodium tamari

1 tablespoon balsamic vinegar

BALSAMIC DIPPING SAUCE

2 tablespoons extra-virgin olive oil

1 tablespoon balsamic vinegar

½ teaspoon brown sugar

½ teaspoon prepared mustard

1 clove garlic, minced

Sea salt

Freshly ground pepper

To prepare the artichokes, put 2 to 4 inches of water in a deep saucepan large enough to hold all the artichokes snugly so they remain upright as they cook. Put the artichokes in the pan and bring to a boil over medium-high heat. Decrease the heat to medium, cover, and cook for 25 to 30 minutes, until tender, rotating the artichokes halfway through the cooking time. They are done when an outer leaf peels off easily.

Drain and let cool slightly. Cut the artichokes in half vertically. Scoop out the fuzzy center choke with a teaspoon. Let cool for at least 1 hour, or wrap tightly in plastic wrap and refrigerate for up to 1 day.

About 10 minutes before serving, heat the oil in a large skillet over medium heat. Put the artichokes in the skillet cut-side down and drizzle the tamari over them. Cook until just starting to brown, 3 to 5 minutes. Turn and cook the other side until just starting to brown, 3 to 5 minutes. Add a bit of water to deglaze the pan. Turn the artichokes again so the cut side faces down. Add the vinegar and simmer until the liquid is reduced and the artichokes are glazed and browned, about 2 minutes. Turn again and cook the other side until browned, about 2 minutes, adding a bit of water or oil as needed to prevent sticking.

Meanwhile, to prepare the dipping sauce, put the oil, vinegar, brown sugar, mustard, and garlic in a small bowl and whisk to combine. Season with salt and pepper to taste.

Serve the artichokes warm, with the dipping sauce alongside in small bowls.

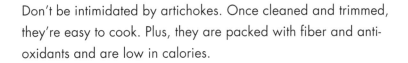

Don't be intimidated by artichokes. Once cleaned and trimmed, they're easy to cook. Plus, they are packed with fiber and anti-oxidants and are low in calories.

Easy Artichokes with Lemon Dipping Sauce

MAKES 4 SERVINGS

ARTICHOKES

½ onion, sliced

1 tablespoon balsamic, cider, or red wine vinegar

4 artichokes, trimmed (see note)

LEMON DIPPING SAUCE

½ cup vegan margarine

1 to 2 teaspoons freshly squeezed lemon juice

Sea salt

To prepare the artichokes, put 3 to 4 inches of water in a deep saucepan large enough to hold all the artichokes snugly so they remain upright as they cook. Add the onion and vinegar. Put the artichokes in the pan and bring to a boil over medium-high heat. Decrease the heat to medium, cover, and cook until the artichokes are tender, 25 to 30 minutes, rotating the artichokes halfway through the cooking time. They are done when an outer leaf peels off easily.

Meanwhile, to make the sauce, melt the margarine in a small saucepan over medium-low heat. Remove from the heat and stir in the lemon juice. Season with salt to taste.

Serve the artichokes warm, with the dipping sauce alongside in small bowls.

NOTE: If you haven't been fortunate enough to enjoy freshly cooked artichokes, you may feel stymied about how to eat them. Simply pull off the leaves one at a time, starting with the outermost leaves near the bottom of the artichoke. Draw the base of the leaf through your clenched teeth to scrape off the soft portion, and discard the rest of the leaf. As you progress upward from the base, the leaves will become more tender, with larger edible portions. When you reach the hairy choke, remove and discard it using a teaspoon. What remains is the artichoke heart, which you can then cut and eat. Be sure to provide empty bowls at the table for discarding the inedible part of the leaves.

This side dish is hearty enough to serve as an entrée. For a simple but satisfying summer supper, pair it with crusty bread or cooked quinoa.

Spinach with Garbanzo Beans and Caramelized Onion

2 teaspoons extra-virgin olive oil

1 sweet onion, chopped

1 teaspoon reduced-sodium tamari, plus more as needed

½ teaspoon brown sugar

1 large bunch spinach, very thinly sliced

⅛ to ¼ teaspoon crushed red pepper flakes

1 can (15 ounces) garbanzo beans, drained and rinsed

Heat the oil in a large skillet over medium heat. Add the onion and cook, stirring occasionally, until translucent, about 8 minutes, adding water, 1 teaspoon at a time, as needed to prevent sticking. Decrease the heat to medium-low. Add the tamari and brown sugar and cook, stirring occasionally, until the onion is very tender and lightly browned, 10 to 15 minutes. Add the spinach and crushed red pepper flakes and cook, stirring frequently, until the spinach begins to wilt. Add the garbanzo beans and cook, stirring occasionally, until the spinach wilts and the garbanzo beans are heated through, about 3 minutes, adding water or additional tamari, 1 teaspoon at a time, as needed to prevent sticking. Serve immediately.

Jazzy Tip Eating more vegetarian meals is not only healthier for us but also better for the environment. The Environmental Defense Fund estimates that if every American replaced one meal of chicken per week with plant-based options, the reduction in carbon dioxide emissions would be the same as taking more than half a million cars off of US roads.

Here I've jazzed up mashed potatoes with cauliflower, giving the dish a boost in nutrients, especially vitamin C, while also making it lower in calories. Because cauliflower has a mellow flavor and creamy texture, the result is much like the traditional version of the ever-popular side dish. Although the potatoes are sharing the stage, they still play an important role, holding everything together after mashing.

Mashed Potatoes and Cauliflower

MAKES 4 TO 5 SERVINGS

1 head cauliflower, coarsely chopped

2 medium white potatoes, peeled and coarsely chopped

¼ cup unsweetened nondairy milk, plus more as needed

1 tablespoon vegan margarine, plus more as needed

½ teaspoon italian herbs

¼ teaspoon sea salt

Freshly ground pepper

Chopped fresh parsley or basil, for garnish

Steam the cauliflower and potatoes until soft but not mushy, about 15 minutes.

Meanwhile, heat the nondairy milk in a small saucepan over medium-low heat until steaming hot but not boiling.

Transfer the cauliflower and potatoes to a medium bowl and add the nondairy milk, margarine, italian herbs, and salt. Mash with a potato masher until smooth and lump-free, adding more nondairy milk or margarine as needed to achieve the desired consistency. Season with pepper to taste. Serve immediately, garnished with parsley if desired.

This dish is a fun and colorful change of pace from standard mashed potatoes, and because of the addition of carrots, it also has a more well-rounded nutritional profile.

Mashed Carrots and Potatoes with Rosemary

6 large carrots, peeled and chopped

4 small potatoes, peeled and chopped

¼ cup unsweetened nondairy milk, plus more as needed

1 tablespoon vegan margarine, plus more as needed

1 teaspoon crushed dried rosemary

Sea salt

Freshly ground black pepper

Steam the carrots and potatoes until soft but not mushy, about 15 minutes.

Meanwhile, heat the nondairy milk in a small saucepan over medium-low heat until steaming hot but not boiling.

Transfer the carrots and potatoes to a medium bowl and add the nondairy milk, margarine, and rosemary. Mash with a potato masher until smooth and lump-free, adding more nondairy milk or margarine as needed to achieve the desired consistency. Season with salt and pepper to taste. Serve immediately.

NOTE: I love the taste of rosemary, but not everyone does. If you prefer, you can substitute basil, oregano, or parsley, using 1 tablespoon of chopped fresh herbs or 1 teaspoon dried.

This simple side dish works well as an antipasto appetizer or as part of a buffet. Roasting the peppers imbues them with an intoxicating sweet-and-smoky flavor that pairs well with many dishes.

Basil Roasted Peppers

MAKES 4 TO 6 SERVINGS

6 large colored bell peppers (red, orange, yellow, or a combination), **each cut into 4 or 5 pieces**
½ **cup chopped fresh basil, or 2½ tablespoons dried**
1 tablespoon extra-virgin olive oil, plus more as needed
¼ **teaspoon sea salt**

Preheat the oven to 400 degrees F. Line a large, rimmed baking sheet with parchment paper.

Put the peppers, basil, oil, and salt in a large bowl. Toss to sparingly coat the peppers with the oil, adding a bit more oil if needed. Spread the peppers in a single layer on the lined baking sheet, skin-side up. Bake for 20 to 25 minutes, until soft to the touch and slightly browned along the edges.

Let cool for at least 10 minutes. Serve hot, at room temperature, or chilled.

This straightforward recipe produces baked potatoes with a flavorful and crispy potato crust and a fluffy interior. Russet potatoes are the spud of choice here, but this recipe also works well with red, yukon gold, or white potatoes.

Baked Potatoes Encrusted with Olive Oil and Sea Salt

MAKES 4 SERVINGS

4 large russet potatoes, scrubbed

2 teaspoons extra-virgin olive oil

1 teaspoon coarse sea salt

Preheat the oven to 400 degrees F. Line a small, rimmed baking sheet with parchment paper.

Carve an X on the top of each potato to allow steam to escape during baking. Put the potatoes in a large bowl and sprinkle with the oil and salt. Using your hands or a large spoon, toss the potatoes until lightly coated. Transfer to the lined baking sheet. Bake for about 1 hour, until crispy on the outside and slightly soft when squeezed (use oven mitts!). Serve immediately.

NOTE: Top the potatoes with your favorite condiments: salsa, onions, catsup, or mustard. Some other great toppers are Jazzy Black Bean Chili (page 135), Spinach with Garbanzo Beans and Caramelized Onion (page 157), or Baked Beans Marinara (page 168).

If you're a fan of french fries but could do without the fat and calories of deep-fried versions, you'll love this recipe. Although these oven-roasted potatoes have only 1 tablespoon of oil in the entire recipe, they have a crispy exterior that's extra crunchy because the potatoes aren't peeled. Don't forget the catsup!

Fabulous Oven Fries

MAKES 2 TO 4 SERVINGS

4 medium russet potatoes, scrubbed

1 tablespoon extra-virgin olive oil

½ to 1 teaspoon chili powder (optional)

½ teaspoon sea salt

Preheat the oven to 400 degrees F. Line a large, rimmed baking sheet with parchment paper.

Cut the potatoes into matchsticks; the thinner they are, the crispier the fries will be. Put the potatoes, oil, optional chili powder, and salt in a large bowl and toss gently until the potatoes are evenly coated. Spread the potatoes in a single layer on the lined baking sheet. Bake for 25 to 35 minutes, until soft inside, slightly crisp outside, and browning along the edges. Serve immediately.

These baked zucchini "fries" are super satisfying and make an ideal accompaniment to any sandwich, such as Reuben-Style Sandwiches (page 84) or Eggless Egg Salad Sandwiches (see page 102). They stand in well for conventional french fries, but you'll have no guilt about eating this delightful squash-based substitute.

Zesty Zucchini Oven Fries

3 zucchini

1 tablespoon extra-virgin olive oil

½ to 1 teaspoon chili powder

½ teaspoon sea salt

Several grinds freshly ground pepper

Preheat the oven to 425 degrees F. Line a large, rimmed baking sheet with foil and lightly oil the foil.

Cut the zucchini into thick matchsticks. Put the zucchini, oil, chili powder, salt, and pepper in a large bowl and toss gently until the zucchini is evenly coated. Spread the zucchini in a single layer on the lined baking sheet. Bake for 20 to 25 minutes, until slightly crisp and browning along the edges. Serve immediately.

This dish pairs well with many entrées and also makes a great addition to any holiday meal. As a bonus, it can be ready in thirty minutes or less.

Maple Sweet Potatoes

see photo, page 124

3 medium sweet potatoes or yams, peeled and cubed

2 tablespoons vegan margarine, plus more as needed

1 tablespoon maple syrup

¼ to ½ teaspoon pumpkin pie spice

¼ teaspoon sea salt

Steam the sweet potatoes until soft, 20 to 25 minutes. Transfer to a large bowl. Add the margarine, maple syrup, pumpkin pie spice, and salt. Mash with a potato masher until smooth, adding a bit more margarine if the potatoes seem dry. Serve immediately.

The winter holidays call for a sweet potato or yam casserole, and you can use either in this dish. This casserole is best assembled well before baking so the yams become infused with the flavors of the maple syrup and spices. For a wonderful pairing, try this dish with Crispy Portobello Steaks (page 128) or Perfect Party Portobellos (page 144).

Yam Casserole

6 medium yams or sweet potatoes, peeled and sliced ¼ to ½ inch thick

3 tablespoons maple syrup

1 tablespoon extra-virgin olive oil

½ teaspoon garlic powder

½ teaspoon pumpkin pie spice

⅛ teaspoon sea salt

Pinch cayenne

½ cup walnuts or pecan halves

Steam the yams until crisp-tender, about 10 minutes. Transfer to a large bowl. Add 1 tablespoon of the maple syrup and the oil, garlic powder, pumpkin pie spice, salt, and cayenne. Toss gently until the yams are evenly coated. Arrange the yams in overlapping layers in a 13 x 9-inch baking pan. Scatter the walnuts over the top, then drizzle with the remaining maple syrup. Cover and refrigerate for 2 to 4 hours if time permits.

Put the pan in a cold oven. Set the heat to 400 degrees F and bake for 40 to 50 minutes, until the yams are tender and browning around the edges.

Let cool for 10 to 15 minutes. Serve warm.

Baking the garlic before adding it to the asparagus gives this dish a mellow, sweet flavor that isn't overly garlicky. The tomatoes add texture and also complement the vibrant green color of the delicate asparagus spears.

Roasted Asparagus with Garlic and Tomatoes

see photo, page 124   **MAKES 4 SERVINGS**

2 cloves garlic, chopped

3 teaspoons extra-virgin olive oil

1 large bunch slender asparagus spears, trimmed

¼ to ½ teaspoon sea salt

10 to 15 cherry or grape tomatoes

Preheat the oven to 400 degrees F. Line a large, rimmed baking sheet with parchment paper.

Put the garlic in the center of a 12-inch square of aluminum foil. Drizzle with 1 teaspoon of the oil. Wrap the garlic in the foil, crimping the edges to make a tight seal. Bake for 15 to 20 minutes, until golden and soft.

Meanwhile, put the asparagus in a large bowl. Drizzle with the remaining 2 teaspoons of oil and sprinkle with the salt. Toss gently until the asparagus is evenly coated.

Spread the asparagus in a single layer on the lined baking sheet. Unwrap the garlic (carefully, as it will be very hot). Distribute the garlic over the asparagus. Bake for 5 to 10 minutes, depending on the thickness of the asparagus. Scatter the tomatoes over the asparagus and bake for 3 to 5 minutes, until the asparagus is crisp-tender but not mushy.

Arrange the asparagus on a serving platter and spoon the garlic and tomatoes over the top. Serve hot, warm, or chilled.

This recipe comes together quickly if you purchase precut butternut squash, which is often available in supermarkets. The squash and garlic are slightly browned and caramelized due to the long roasting time, producing a naturally sweet side dish that pairs well with many entrées.

Roasted Butternut Squash with Garlic

MAKES 2 TO 4 SERVINGS

1 medium butternut squash, peeled and cubed (3 to 4 cups)

8 to 10 cloves garlic, coarsely chopped

1 teaspoon extra-virgin olive oil

Sea salt

Freshly ground pepper

Preheat the oven to 375 degrees F. Line a large, rimmed baking sheet with parchment paper.

Put the squash, garlic, and oil in a medium bowl and toss to combine. Spread the mixture in a single layer on the lined baking sheet. Bake for 45 to 55 minutes, until tender, turning once or twice during baking. Season with salt and pepper to taste. Serve immediately.

Cauliflower is a cruciferous vegetable and a nutritional superstar, so I am always coming up with new ways to prepare it. This dish is especially good served with a main-course salad.

Roasted Cauliflower with Garlic

MAKES 4 TO 6 SERVINGS

1 head cauliflower, cut into bite-sized florets

2 onions, chopped

8 cloves garlic, chopped

½ teaspoon ground turmeric

½ teaspoon italian seasoning

½ teaspoon dried rosemary

1 to 2 tablespoons extra-virgin olive oil

Sea salt

Freshly ground pepper

Preheat the oven to 400 degrees. Line a large, rimmed baking sheet with parchment paper.

Put the cauliflower, onions, garlic, turmeric, italian seasoning, and rosemary in a large bowl and toss with just enough of the oil to lightly coat the cauliflower. Spread the mixture on the lined baking sheet. Bake for about 45 minutes, until the cauliflower is tender but still holds its shape. Season with salt and pepper to taste. Serve immediately.

The marinara sauce gives these baked beans an Italian flair, while the streamlined prep and use of pantry staples make them the ideal choice when company drops in unexpectedly.

Baked Beans Marinara

MAKES 2 TO 3 SERVINGS

1 can (15 ounces) **white or black beans, drained and rinsed**

1½ cups **jarred marinara sauce**

1 small **sweet onion, chopped**

2 tablespoons **brown sugar**

1 tablespoon **extra-virgin olive oil**

2 cloves **garlic, minced, or** ¼ teaspoon **garlic powder**

⅛ teaspoon **cayenne**

Preheat the oven to 375 degrees F.

Put all the ingredients in a medium bowl and stir until thoroughly combined. Transfer to an 8-inch square glass or ceramic baking pan and spread in an even layer.

Cover with foil and bake for about 45 minutes, until bubbling hot, uncovering for the last 10 minutes to brown the top if desired. Serve immediately.

A delicious vegan stuffing is a must-have for a spectacular holiday meal. When baked on its own, this version is moist on the inside, crispy on the outside, and guaranteed to satisfy. It's also the perfect filling for Stuffed Acorn Squash (page 137).

Mushroom, Walnut, and Celery Stuffing

7 slices sprouted whole-grain bread or other whole-grain bread, diced

1 teaspoon italian seasoning

½ teaspoon sea salt

1 tablespoon extra-virgin olive oil

1 sweet onion, chopped

2 stalks celery, with leaves, diced

2½ cups diced cremini or white button mushrooms

1 teaspoon reduced-sodium tamari

¼ cup vegan margarine

½ cup boiling water

1 vegetable bouillon cube

1 cup finely chopped walnuts

Preheat the oven to 375 degrees F. Oil an 11 x 7-inch baking pan.

Put the bread, italian seasoning, and salt in a medium bowl and toss to combine. Transfer to a large, rimmed baking sheet and bake for 8 to 10 minutes, until the bread is slightly crisp.

Meanwhile, heat the oil in a large skillet over medium heat. Add the onion and celery and cook, stirring occasionally, until the onion is translucent, 8 to 10 minutes. Add the mushrooms and tamari and cook, stirring occasionally, until the mushrooms are tender, adding a bit of water as needed to prevent sticking.

Melt the margarine in a small saucepan over medium heat. Put the water in a small bowl or measuring cup and add the bouillon cube. Stir until dissolved to make a strong vegetable broth.

Put the bread and walnuts in a large bowl and toss until well combined. Add the mushroom mixture, margarine, and ¼ cup of the broth and stir gently until thoroughly combined. Add as much of the remaining broth as needed so the mixture is moist but not soupy. If the mixture still seems dry after adding all of the broth, add a small amount of water. Transfer to the prepared pan. Spread in an even layer and smooth the top with a spatula.

Cover and bake for about 30 minutes. Uncover and bake for 15 minutes to crisp the top. Serve immediately.

When you want an easy but jazzy way to serve bread, give this flavorful option a try. Offer it as a starter, as so many restaurants do, or serve it with soups, salads, or main dishes.

Warm Bakery Bread with Herbed Dipping Oil

MAKES 6 TO 8 SERVINGS

1 loaf crusty whole-grain bread

3 to 4 tablespoons extra-virgin olive oil

3 cloves garlic, minced, or ½ teaspoon garlic powder

1 teaspoon italian seasoning

Preheat the oven to 400 degrees F.

Tightly wrap the bread in foil. Bake for 15 to 20 minutes, until heated through.

Meanwhile, put the oil, garlic, and italian seasoning in a small bowl and stir until thoroughly combined.

Slice the bread and serve it in a bread basket or large bowl, wrapped in a large cloth napkin to keep it warm. Serve immediately, with the oil mixture alongside in small bowls.

This recipe is based on my grandmother's version, which was always a favorite of mine. I've updated it to use fresh garlic and whole-grain bread, as it's more nutritious and hearty. This tantalizing loaf, with its crispy crust and herbed, soft, and steamy inside, is bursting with flavor. In other words . . . perfection!

Grandma's Garlic Bread

MAKES 10 TO 12 SERVINGS

1 large loaf whole-grain italian bread

½ cup vegan margarine, at room temperature

6 to 8 cloves garlic, minced

1 tablespoon italian seasoning (see note)

Preheat the oven to 400 degrees F.

Put the bread on a cutting board. Use a serrated bread knife to slice ½- to 1-inch-thick slices diagonally across the entire loaf, but don't cut all the way through the bottom crust; leave the bottom of the loaf intact.

Put the margarine, garlic, and italian seasoning in a small bowl and mash with the back of a fork until thoroughly combined. Working carefully so as not to separate the slices, spread the margarine mixture on each side of each slice. Wrap tightly in foil, crimping the edges to form a tight seal (see note).

Bake for 20 to 25 minutes, until the crust is crispy and the interior is hot and steamy. Remove the foil and serve the bread in a bread basket or large bowl, wrapped in a large cloth napkin to keep it warm.

NOTES

- If you have fresh herbs such as basil or oregano on hand, feel free to substitute about 3 tablespoons of minced fresh herbs for the italian seasoning, or add them along with the dried herbs.

- Once the bread is wrapped in foil, it may be stored in a ziplock bag in the refrigerator for 3 to 4 hours before baking.

Decadent Desserts and Beverages

Pots de Crème, 178

Serving a tasty vegan dessert need not be challenging. Fruit-based desserts can be a light, refreshing option, not to mention quick and easy, and I've included a few in this chapter. But that's just the beginning. Don't imagine that adhering to a plant-based diet means forgoing baked goods and other *decadent delights.* There are many high-quality vegan ingredients that you can easily substitute for the eggs and dairy products usually associated with these culinary creations. Best of all, these substitutions typically result in desserts that are *lower in fat and calories* yet still delightfully delicious—and often more nutritious. Using nondairy milk in place of cow's milk is straightforward, but replacing eggs is less so. Some of the recipes in this chapter include mashed bananas for binding, whereas others use nut butters, blended tofu, or vegan cream cheese to fill this role. The result is recipes that are *easy on your waistline* and guilt-free. Now you can feel great about surprising your family and friends with delectable *homemade confections.* By the way, I've also included a couple of recipes for my favorite summertime sippers. Enjoy!

In this delectable dessert with a true Italian flair, the tart balsamic vinegar combines with the sweet brown sugar to produce a thick syrup that flavors and coats tender strawberries. This dish is wonderfully light and refreshing.

Balsamic Strawberry Delight

2 cups (1 pint) strawberries, halved

2 tablespoons brown sugar

1 tablespoon balsamic vinegar

Put all the ingredients in a medium bowl and stir gently until thoroughly combined. Cover and let sit at room temperature for about 30 minutes. Serve at room temperature or chilled.

A hint of chili powder gives this fluffy dark chocolate pudding peppery undertones, while cinnamon adds sweet, earthy notes, making it the ideal finish to any spicy meal. Chocolate lovers rejoice!

Sweet-and-Spicy Chocolate Mousse

MAKES 4 SERVINGS

1 cup vanilla nondairy milk

3½ ounces vegan dark chocolate, broken into ¼- to ½-inch pieces

1 tablespoon maple syrup

¼ teaspoon ground cinnamon

¼ teaspoon chili powder

¼ teaspoon vanilla extract

Heat the nondairy milk in a small saucepan over medium-low heat until steaming hot but not boiling.

Put the chocolate in a blender, then add the maple syrup, cinnamon, chili powder, and vanilla extract. Pour in the nondairy milk and process until smooth and frothy, stopping twice to scrape down the sides of the blender jar.

Spoon the mixture into four dessert cups or wine glasses and refrigerate until set, at least 3 hours. Serve chilled.

This dessert sounds fancy, but it's a breeze to prepare. Especially refreshing as an afternoon snack or light dessert in warmer weather, this creamy concoction emulates frozen custard and is much more economical than store-bought nondairy versions. Note that to achieve the ideal consistency, the bananas should be frozen for at least twenty-four hours before making this dessert and the nondairy milk should be well chilled.

Frozen Banana Creamy with Cocoa Dust

MAKES 2 SERVINGS

3 large frozen bananas (see note, page 40)

1½ cups chilled vanilla nondairy milk

3 to 4 teaspoons brown sugar or maple syrup

1 teaspoon unsweetened cocoa powder

Put the bananas, nondairy milk, and brown sugar in a blender and process until smooth and creamy.

Pour the mixture into pretty dessert dishes or glasses. Sprinkle with the cocoa powder and serve immediately.

This delectably smooth and frosty dessert is a beautiful way to end any meal, and it comes together in just five minutes. It is a lighter alternative to traditional puddings, as it uses tofu rather than eggs and cream. For added elegance and indulgence, serve vegan tea cookies with the parfaits.

Luscious Raspberry Parfaits

MAKES 3 SERVINGS

2¼ cups frozen raspberries

8 ounces soft regular or silken tofu, drained

3 tablespoons maple syrup

¼ to ½ teaspoon vanilla extract

Put 5 or 6 raspberries in three champagne glasses or glass dessert dishes. Set aside 3 of the remaining raspberries for garnish. Put the tofu, maple syrup, vanilla extract, and remaining raspberries in a blender or food processor and process until smooth and creamy.

Spoon the mixture into the glasses or dessert dishes and garnish each with a raspberry. Serve immediately.

This delicate, rich dessert is based on a recipe my grandma often made. When I was a child it was my favorite dessert, but it was packed with eggs and heavy cream. Here's a fail-safe vegan version that faithfully reproduces the taste of Grandma's specialty. Served in tiny espresso cups, it provides an elegant ending to any fancy meal. Plus, you can make it the day before serving if you wish—always a bonus when entertaining.

Pots de Crème

MAKES 4 TO 6 SERVINGS

¾ cup vanilla nondairy milk

12 ounces soft regular or silken tofu, drained and cubed

2 teaspoons brown sugar

1 cup vegan dark chocolate chips

Heat the nondairy milk in a small saucepan over medium-low heat until steaming hot but not boiling.

Put the tofu and brown sugar in a blender, then add the chocolate chips. Pour in the nondairy milk and process until completely smooth.

Spoon the mixture into tiny dessert bowls or espresso cups and refrigerate for 4 to 24 hours. Serve chilled.

This is the easiest and tastiest chocolate pudding recipe you'll ever savor. It takes under ten minutes to prepare but will garner oohs and aahs every time you serve it. It is rich, thick, and decadent and will satisfy even the most dedicated chocoholic on your guest list.

Chocolate Ganache Pudding

MAKES 4 SERVINGS

1 cup vanilla nondairy milk

5 ounces vegan dark chocolate, finely chopped

2 teaspoons brown sugar

2 teaspoons unsweetened cocoa powder, for garnish

Heat the nondairy milk in a small saucepan over medium-low heat until steaming hot but not boiling.

Put the chocolate and brown sugar in a medium bowl. Slowly pour in the nondairy milk, about ⅓ cup at a time, and whisk vigorously after each addition until smooth and shiny.

Spoon the mixture into four tiny dessert bowls or espresso cups and refrigerate until set, at least 4 hours. To serve, place each cup on a small plate or saucer and sprinkle the pudding with about ½ teaspoon of the cocoa powder if desired.

These rich and decadent-tasting vegan confections are simple to make. And because they are best when prepared in advance, they're a great dessert to serve when entertaining guests.

Chocolate Truffle Trio

7 ounces vegan dark chocolate (70 to 85 percent cacao)

½ cup brown sugar

¼ cup plain or vanilla nondairy milk

¼ teaspoon vanilla extract

Pinch cayenne (optional)

¼ cup confectioners' sugar, for coating

¼ cup unsweetened cocoa powder, for coating

¼ cup finely chopped walnuts or other nuts, for coating

Put the chocolate and brown sugar in a double boiler over medium-low heat (see note). When the chocolate has melted, remove from the heat. Add the nondairy milk, vanilla extract, and optional cayenne and whisk until thick and shiny. Transfer to a medium bowl and refrigerate just until cool enough to handle, about 15 minutes.

Meanwhile, line a baking sheet with parchment paper. Put the confectioners' sugar, cocoa powder, and walnuts in three separate small bowls. Spoon out 1 tablespoon of the chocolate mixture and quickly roll it into a ball. Roll it in the confectioners' sugar until completely coated. Continue in this way, forming the chocolate mixture into balls and coating one-third of them in the confectioners' sugar, one-third in the cocoa powder, and one-third in the walnuts.

Arrange the balls in a single layer on the lined baking sheet. Cover and refrigerate until set, about 4 hours.

Let the truffles soften at room temperature for 30 minutes before serving. Stored in an airtight container in the refrigerator, the truffles will keep for 4 to 5 days.

NOTE: If you don't have a double boiler, you can improvise one with a heatproof bowl and a saucepan. The bowl should partially (not completely)

fit into the saucepan. Fill the saucepan with enough water so that when the bowl rests in the saucepan the water doesn't touch the bottom of the bowl. Bring the water to a simmer. Put the ingredients in the bowl and place it in the saucepan.

VARIATION: Unsweetened shredded dried coconut may be used instead of or in addition to the other truffle coatings.

Although this fudge is a rich treat and fills the bill when a decadent dessert is called for, it's full of healthful ingredients, making it a fun afternoon snack for kids and adults alike.

Peanut Butter Fudge

MAKES 16 PIECES, OR 8 TO 10 SERVINGS

¾ cup smooth or chunky peanut butter

⅓ cup maple syrup

3½ ounces vegan dark chocolate

⅓ cup unsalted roasted sunflower seeds

¼ cup raisins

Lightly coat an 8-inch square baking pan with vegan margarine.

Put the peanut butter and maple syrup in a large bowl and stir vigorously until well combined.

Melt the chocolate in a double boiler over medium-low heat (see note, pages 180–181). Pour the chocolate into the peanut butter mixture and stir until thoroughly combined. Fold in the sunflower seeds and raisins. Transfer to the prepared pan. Spread in an even layer and smooth the top. Score the surface at 2-inch intervals with a table knife; this will make it easier to cut the fudge after it has set.

Cover with foil and refrigerate until firm enough that the fudge holds its shape when cut, about 30 minutes. Serve chilled. Stored in an airtight container in the refrigerator, the fudge will keep for about 1 week.

PEANUT BUTTER AND COCONUT FUDGE: Fold in ⅓ cup of flaked coconut with the sunflower seeds and raisins.

DOUBLE-ALMOND FUDGE: Substitute almond butter for the peanut butter and chopped roasted almonds for the sunflower seeds.

DOUBLE-CASHEW FUDGE: Substitute cashew butter for the peanut butter and chopped roasted cashews for the sunflower seeds.

These cookies have an appealing crispy crunch, along with an enticing almond flavor thanks to almond butter, which acts as a binder, and almond milk. For a triple-almond treat, serve them with a tall glass of cold almond milk.

Almondy Oatmeal Cookies with Raisins and Chocolate Chips

MAKES 15 TO 20 COOKIES

¾ cup rolled oats

½ cup whole wheat flour

½ teaspoon baking powder

¼ teaspoon sea salt

½ cup brown sugar

⅓ cup vegan margarine, at room temperature

3 tablespoons almond butter

½ teaspoon vanilla extract

¼ cup almond milk, plus more as needed

½ cup raisins

½ cup vegan dark chocolate chips

Preheat the oven to 350 degrees F. Line two baking sheets with parchment paper.

Put the oats, flour, baking powder, and salt in a large bowl and stir with a dry whisk to combine. Put the brown sugar and margarine in a medium bowl and stir vigorously until smooth and well combined. Add the almond butter and vanilla extract and stir vigorously until smooth and well blended. Add to the oat mixture, along with the almond milk, to make a dough. Stir until well combined. The dough will be stiff, but if it seems overly dry, stir in a bit more nondairy milk, 1 tablespoon at a time. Fold in the raisins and chocolate chips.

For each cookie, drop 1 heaping tablespoonful of the dough onto the lined baking sheets, spacing them 2 inches apart. Flatten slightly with a spatula. Bake for 15 to 18 minutes, until golden brown, rotating the baking sheets halfway through the baking time.

Put the baking sheets on a wire rack. Let the cookies cool on the baking sheets for about 15 minutes before transferring to a serving platter or storage container. Stored in an airtight container in the refrigerator, the cookies will keep for 7 to 10 days.

Jazzy Tip I love using parchment paper, which makes any pan nonstick, even with the stickiest baked goods. Because it eliminates the need to oil pans, it makes cleanup much speedier. Plus, it's compostable! Opt for unbleached parchment paper. This way it's a chlorine-free product—better for you, and better for the environment.

This cake makes an impressive holiday dessert, especially when topped with Maple Tofu Whip (page 193), and is also a festive offering at breakfast or brunch. Instead of relying on heavily dyed and sugared candied fruits as so many fruitcakes do, it gets its rich taste from luscious dates, crunchy walnuts, tart apples, and earthy spices. Don't be put off by the lengthy list of ingredients; this cake only takes about twenty minutes to assemble.

Fruit and Nut Spice Cake

MAKES 6 TO 8 SERVINGS

TOPPING

1 apple, peeled, cored, and diced

⅓ cup chopped walnuts

2 tablespoons brown rice syrup, or 1½ tablespoons maple syrup

1 teaspoon vegetable oil

½ teaspoon ground cinnamon

CAKE

2 cups whole wheat flour

1 tablespoon baking powder

¾ teaspoon pumpkin pie spice

½ teaspoon ground cinnamon

⅛ teaspoon sea salt

½ cup brown sugar

⅓ cup chopped walnuts

¼ cup raisins

5 large medjool dates, pitted and diced

1¼ cups plain or vanilla nondairy milk

1 ripe banana, mashed until smooth

¼ cup vegetable oil

Preheat the oven to 375 degrees F. Line an 8 x 4-inch loaf pan with parchment paper, with a 2- to 3-inch overhang on all four sides of the pan.

To make the topping, put all the ingredients in a medium bowl and stir gently until thoroughly combined. Transfer to the prepared pan, spreading the mixture in an even layer and pressing it firmly.

To make the cake, put the flour, baking powder, ½ teaspoon of the pumpkin pie spice, and the cinnamon and salt in a large bowl and stir with a dry whisk to combine. Add the brown sugar and stir with the whisk to combine. Add the walnuts, raisins, and dates and stir until coated with the flour. Add the nondairy milk, banana, oil, and the remaining ¼ teaspoon pumpkin pie spice and stir until smooth and lump-free.

Pour the mixture into the lined pan and smooth the top. Fold the sides of the parchment paper upward to form a collar around the cake, which will give it support as it rises during baking.

Bake for 45 to 55 minutes, until firm to the touch and a toothpick inserted in the center comes out clean.

Put the pan on a wire rack. Let cool for 15 minutes. Invert onto a serving platter and carefully peel off the parchment paper. Let cool for 10 minutes longer before slicing. Serve warm or at room temperature. Wrapped tightly and refrigerated, leftover cake will keep for about 4 days.

To bind the ingredients, this cake uses store-bought vegan cream cheese, which also adds moisture without making the cake heavy. Note that the frosting must be made in advance so it can be refrigerated for at least an hour to set up, so plan ahead. In a pinch you could also top the cake with a dusting of confectioners' sugar.

Double-Chocolate Cake

2 cups whole wheat pastry flour

⅔ cup unsweetened cocoa powder

1 teaspoon baking powder

1 teaspoon baking soda

½ teaspoon sea salt

1 to 1¼ cups brown sugar (use the larger amount for a sweeter cake)

1½ cups chocolate nondairy milk, plus more as needed

¼ cup vegan cream cheese, at room temperature

¼ cup vegetable oil

1 teaspoon vanilla extract

Vegan Cream Cheese Frosting (see page 50)

Preheat the oven to 400 degrees F. Lightly coat an 8-inch square baking pan with vegan margarine.

Put the flour, cocoa powder, baking powder, baking soda, and salt in a large bowl and stir with a dry whisk to combine. Add the brown sugar and stir with the whisk to combine.

Put ¼ cup of the nondairy milk and the vegan cream cheese, oil, and vanilla extract in a medium bowl and stir vigorously until fairly smooth (it's fine if flecks of vegan cream cheese are still visible). Add to the flour mixture, along with the remaining 1¼ cups of nondairy milk. Stir until well combined and somewhat fluffy. The mixture will be stiff, but if it seems overly dry, stir in additional nondairy milk (up to 3 tablespoons), 1 tablespoon at a time.

Pour the mixture into the prepared pan and smooth the top. Bake for 15 minutes. Decrease the heat to 350 degrees F and bake for about 25 minutes, until a toothpick inserted in the center comes out clean. If it seems that the cake is starting to burn during the last 10 minutes of baking, tent it with foil.

Put the pan on a wire rack. Let cool completely. Spread the frosting evenly over the top. Covered tightly and stored in the refrigerator, leftover cake will keep for about 4 days.

VARIATION: If double chocolate seems over the top, substitute vanilla nondairy milk for the chocolate variety.

Pineapple keeps this cake moist, and pecans add a wonderful taste and texture, making for a mouthwatering dessert, especially when served topped with a dollop of Maple Tofu Whip (page 193). However, it isn't overly sweet, so it can do double duty as an indulgent breakfast, perhaps served with vegan yogurt on the side.

Pineapple-Pecan Cake

MAKES 6 TO 8 SERVINGS

TOPPING

½ ripe pineapple, cored and thinly sliced

1 tablespoon brown sugar

CAKE

2 cups whole wheat flour

1 tablespoon baking powder

¼ teaspoon sea salt

⅓ to ⅔ cup brown sugar (use the larger amount for a sweeter cake)

2 tablespoons toasted wheat germ

1 cup chopped pecans

1 cup diced fresh pineapple

1¼ cups plain or vanilla nondairy milk

⅓ cup vegetable oil

1 teaspoon vanilla extract

Preheat the oven to 375 degrees F. Lightly spread vegan margarine over the sides of an 8-inch square baking pan, then line the bottom with parchment paper.

To make the topping, put the pineapple slices in a medium bowl and sprinkle with the brown sugar. Turn the slices over gently to evenly coat them with the sugar. Arrange the pineapple slices in a single layer in the prepared pan, slightly overlapping them.

To make the cake, put the flour, baking powder, and salt in a large bowl and stir with a dry whisk to combine. Add the brown sugar and wheat germ and stir with the whisk to combine. Add the pecans and pineapple and stir until coated with the flour. Add the nondairy milk, oil, and vanilla extract and stir just until evenly incorporated and smooth.

Pour the mixture into the prepared pan and smooth the top. Bake for 50 to 60 minutes, until the top is golden and a toothpick inserted in the center comes out clean. If the cake begins to brown too much during the last 15 minutes of baking, tent it with foil.

Put the pan on a wire rack and loosen the sides with a knife. Let cool for about 15 minutes. Invert onto a serving platter and carefully peel off the parchment paper. Let cool for 10 minutes longer before slicing. Serve warm or at room temperature. Wrapped tightly and refrigerated, leftover cake will keep for about 4 days.

I came up with this recipe one fall afternoon after purchasing a big bag of apples from a nearby farm. For extra indulgence, top this scrumptious dessert with Maple Tofu Whip (page 193) or serve nondairy ice cream on the side. If you have any left over, this cake makes a fabulous breakfast treat, whether served cold or rewarmed.

Upside-Down Apple Cake

MAKES 6 TO 8 SERVINGS

TOPPING

3 tablespoons vegan margarine

4 teaspoons brown sugar

¼ teaspoon ground cinnamon

3 apples, peeled, cored, and sliced

CAKE

1 cup whole wheat pastry flour

1 cup whole wheat flour

1 tablespoon baking powder

½ teaspoon sea salt

½ cup brown sugar

1 apple, peeled, cored, and chopped

½ cup raisins

1 cup plain or vanilla nondairy milk

2 ripe bananas, mashed until smooth

¼ cup vegetable oil

GARNISH

Confectioners' sugar or ground cinnamon

Preheat the oven to 375 degrees F. Lightly spread vegan margarine over the sides of an 8-inch square baking pan, then line the bottom with parchment paper.

To make the topping, melt the margarine in a medium skillet over medium heat. Decrease the heat to low and sprinkle in the brown sugar. Cook, stirring constantly, until the mixture thickens slightly and becomes syrupy, about 7 minutes. Remove from the heat and stir in the cinnamon. Add the apples and stir gently until evenly coated. Transfer to the prepared pan, spreading the apples in an even layer.

To make the cake, put the flours, baking powder, and salt in a large bowl and stir with a dry whisk to combine. Add the brown sugar and stir with the whisk to combine. Add the apple and raisins and stir until coated with the flour. Stir in

the nondairy milk, bananas, and oil and mix just until incorporated. Do not overmix or the cake will be tough.

Pour the mixture into the prepared pan and smooth the top. Put the pan on a baking sheet and bake for 45 to 55 minutes, until golden and a toothpick inserted in the center comes out clean. If the cake begins to brown too much during the last 15 minutes of baking, tent it with foil.

Put the pan on a wire rack and loosen the sides with a knife. Let cool for about 15 minutes. Invert onto a serving platter and carefully peel off the parchment paper. Let cool for 10 minutes longer before slicing. Sprinkle the cake with confectioners'

sugar or cinnamon if desired. Serve warm or at room temperature. Wrapped tightly and refrigerated, leftover cake will keep for about 4 days.

If Double-Chocolate Cake (page 185) wasn't chocolaty enough for you, try these moist and gooey treats, which incorporate two types of dark chocolate plus cocoa powder to produce a super-fudgy, triple-chocolate delight. This is one of the best brownie recipes I have ever tasted, vegan or otherwise.

Triple-Chocolate Brownies

2 cups whole wheat flour

1½ cups unsweetened cocoa powder

½ teaspoon sea salt

¼ teaspoon baking powder

1¾ cups brown sugar

2 cups plain or vanilla nondairy milk

12 ounces soft regular or silken tofu, drained

⅔ cup vegan margarine, melted

1¼ cups vegan dark chocolate chips

3½ ounces vegan dark chocolate, chopped

Confectioners' sugar, for dusting (optional)

Preheat the oven to 375 degrees F. Lightly coat a 13 x 9-inch baking pan with vegan margarine.

Put the flour, cocoa powder, salt, and baking powder in a large bowl and stir with a dry whisk to combine. Add the brown sugar and stir with the whisk to combine.

Put the nondairy milk, tofu, and margarine in a blender and process until smooth and creamy. Add to the flour mixture and stir just until incorporated. Fold in the chocolate chips and chocolate. Do not overmix or the brownies will be tough.

Spoon the mixture into the prepared pan and smooth the top. Bake for 45 to 55 minutes, until firm and slightly crusty on top.

Put the pan on a wire rack. Let cool completely before cutting into squares. Transfer to a decora-tive platter and serve dusted with confectioners' sugar if desired. Stored in an airtight container in the refrigerator, leftover brownies will keep for about 4 days.

My grandmother had a big, beautiful apple tree in her backyard, and every fall she made a variety of desserts from its bounty of apples. One of my favorites was her apple crisp. This "veganized" rendition is true to the delicious texture and taste of her version. Top it with vegan ice cream if you like. Although this recipe appears in the desserts chapter, it's nutritious enough to serve for breakfast, doused liberally with nondairy milk.

Autumn Apple Crisp

MAKES 6 TO 8 SERVINGS

4 apples, peeled, cored, and sliced

3 tablespoons raisins

2 tablespoons maple syrup

¼ teaspoon ground cinnamon

1 cup rolled oats

⅓ cup vegan margarine, at room temperature

3 tablespoons unsalted roasted sunflower seeds (optional)

1 tablespoon brown sugar

1 tablespoon whole wheat flour

⅛ teaspoon sea salt

Preheat the oven to 400 degrees F. Lightly coat a 10-inch square baking pan or 12 x 9-inch casserole dish with vegan margarine.

Put the apples, raisins, maple syrup, and cinnamon in a medium bowl and stir gently until well combined. Transfer to the prepared pan, spreading the mixture in an even layer.

Put the oats, margarine, optional sunflower seeds, brown sugar, flour, and salt in a medium bowl and mix with your hands until thoroughly combined. Using your hands or a rubber spatula, spread the mixture evenly over the apples.

Cover and bake for 15 to 20 minutes, until the apples are soft. Uncover and bake for about 10 minutes, until the topping is crisp. Serve warm or at room temperature. Covered tightly and stored in the refrigerator, leftover crisp will keep for about 5 days.

Jazzy Tip When serving a fancy meal, offer a variety of herbal teas as a refreshing accompaniment to the dessert course. Many people don't drink caffeinated beverages, especially at night. I like to offer a number of options in a small wicker basket and pass it around the table so everyone can choose the variety they prefer.

When you feel the need for a whipped cream topping or one of those analogs with unspeakable ingredients, try this creamy tofu whip instead. Its smooth texture and delicate flavor will complement almost any dessert, from frozen concoctions to cakes and pies. It's also great over plain fresh fruit.

Maple Tofu Whip

5 ounces soft regular or silken tofu, drained
¼ cup plain or vanilla nondairy milk
2 tablespoons maple syrup or agave nectar
⅛ teaspoon vanilla extract

Put all the ingredients in a blender or food processor and process until smooth and creamy. Transfer to a bowl, cover, and refrigerate for at least 3 hours, until well chilled. Serve cold. Stored in a covered container in the refrigerator, the topping will keep for 5 to 7 days.

RASPBERRY-MAPLE TOFU WHIP: To imbue this topping with a pretty pink hue, along with a hint of raspberry flavor, add 8 to 12 raspberries before blending.

This rejuvenating sweet-and-spicy tea is the perfect beverage for a hot summer afternoon. For optimum flavor, make it well ahead of time so it can be chilled thoroughly before serving. This will keep the ice from melting quickly and diluting the tea. You can also enjoy this tea in wintertime, served piping hot.

Ginger and Maple Iced Tea

MAKES 4 SERVINGS

2- to 3-inch piece fresh ginger, peeled and minced

1 to 3 tablespoons maple syrup (use the larger amount for a sweeter tea)

4 cups boiling filtered water

Ice cubes

Put the ginger and maple syrup in a teapot. Pour in the water, cover, and let steep for 20 to 30 minutes. Strain through a fine-mesh sieve into a pitcher or jar. Refrigerate for at least 1 hour. To serve, fill four tall glasses with ice. Pour in the tea and serve immediately.

If you need an afternoon pick-me-up, try sipping this cool, refreshing lemonade. It's a sweet twist on an American classic.

Maple Lemonade

MAKES 2 SERVINGS

Juice of 1 large lemon

2½ tablespoons maple syrup

2 to 3 cups ice cubes

3 cups filtered water, or as needed

Put the lemon juice and maple syrup in a small bowl and whisk until thoroughly combined. Pour into two tall glasses, dividing the mixture evenly between them. Add 1 to 1½ cups of ice cubes to each glass. Slowly pour in the water, stirring constantly and filling the glasses to the top. Serve immediately.

Resources

INGREDIENTS AND KITCHEN EQUIPMENT

Bob's Red Mill

bobsredmill.com

Phone: 800-349-2173

Bob's Red Mill sells a wide variety of organic and whole-grain products, including baking aids, beans, flour, grains, hot cereals, nuts, and seeds. They also produce a variety of gluten-free flours and baking products.

Eden Organic

edenfoods.com

Phone: 888-424-3336

Eden Organic offers an expansive array of beans, cereals, miso, nut and seed butters, vegetable oils, whole grains, and more.

Frey Vineyards

freywine.com

Phone: 800-760-3739

Frey Organic Wines are vegan and gluten-free. The wine is also organic and biodynamic, with no sulfites added.

Gold Mine Natural Foods

goldminenaturalfoods.com

Phone: 800-475-3663

Gold Mine Natural Foods distributes traditional macrobiotic foods and hard-to-find organic, heirloom-quality beans, grains, herbs, seeds, and a wide variety of natural pantry items.

Healthy Traders

healthytraders.com

Phone: 888-392-9237

Healthy Traders carries organic and natural foods, kitchen equipment, and cookware, along with a wide variety of essentials for a healthy lifestyle.

Pangea Vegan Products

veganstore.com

Phone: 800-340-1200

Pangea Vegan Products offers a comprehensive selection of high-quality, cruelty-free, and vegan foods, clothing, shoes, and other products.

Penzeys Spices

penzeys.com

Phone: 800-741-7787

Penzeys Spices carries an extensive collection of herbs and spices at reasonable prices.

San-J

Product information: san-j.com

Online store: san-j.elsstore.com

San-J offers tamari soy sauce, reduced-sodium tamari soy sauce, and a variety of Asian cooking sauces, rice crackers, salad dressings, and soups. They also carry gluten-free, certified kosher, and non-GMO tamari.

Trader Joe's

Product information: traderjoes.com

Store locator: traderjoes.com/stores/index.asp

This market chain carries a wide variety of organic and vegan pantry items and produce at low prices.

Vegan Essentials

veganessentials.com

Phone: 866-88-vegan

Vegan Essentials is an online store that is vegan owned and operated. They specialize in animal-free products and provide a one-stop shopping destination for all things vegan.

Wholesome Sweeteners

Product information: wholesomesweeteners.com

Store locator: wholesomesweeteners.com/store_locator.html

Phone: 800-680-1896

Wholesome Sweeteners carries fair-trade, certified organic, and natural sugars that are non-GMO and made without any animal by-products. Their line includes dark and light brown sugars, powdered sugar, organic syrups, Sucanat, and turbinado sugar.

Vitamix

vitamix.com

Phone: 800-848-2649

Vitamix offers rugged blenders for high-performance blending. They are a bit pricey but well worth the investment.

ORGANIZATIONS AND PUBLICATIONS

Go Dairy Free

godairyfree.org

Go Dairy Free is updated daily with cooking tips, food news, product reviews, and recipes. The website offers comprehensive information for milk-free and non-dairy living, featuring a "No Dairy Product List" for grocery shopping needs.

Farm Sanctuary

farmsanctuary.org

Since 1986, Farm Sanctuary has campaigned for legal and policy reforms that promote respect and compassion for farm animals. Their website offers valuable information and links for living cruelty-free through diet and lifestyle.

North American Vegetarian Society (NAVS)

navs-online.org

vegetariansummerfest.org

NAVS strives to inform the public about how vegetarianism benefits humans, other animals, and our shared earth. They have a quarterly magazine, *Vegetarian Voice*, and many publications for individuals with inquiries about living a vegan lifestyle. NAVS also sponsors the annual Vegetarian Summerfest conference.

One Green Planet

onegreenplanet.org

One Green Planet is an online resource that draws links between the world of ecology, the environment, and vegan living. A bounty of vegan recipes is offered and updated regularly.

Physicians Committee for Responsible Medicine (PCRM)

pcrm.org

Founded in 1985, PCRM is a nonprofit organization that promotes preventive medicine, conducts clinical research, and encourages higher standards for ethics and effectiveness in research. Their "New Four Food Groups," which includes fruits, legumes, whole grains, and vegetables, is PCRM's proposal for a federal nutrition policy that puts a new priority on health.

Vegan Baking

veganbaking.net

This site is dedicated to helping vegan bakers by providing a community for those who want a place to compare notes and share knowledge. The website offers a wealth of excellent vegan baking recipes.

VegNews

vegnews.com

VegNews offers readers up-to-date information on living healthfully and compassionately. The website and magazine feature delicious vegan recipes, vegetarian city guides, new vegan products, and much more.

Vegetarian Resource Group (VRG)

vrg.org

VRG is a nonprofit organization dedicated to educating the public about vegetarianism and the interrelated issues of health, nutrition, ecology, ethics, and world hunger. In addition to publishing the quarterly magazine *Vegetarian Journal*, VRG produces and sells cookbooks, other books, pamphlets, and article reprints.

Wellness Forum

wellnessforum.com

The Wellness Forum helps people all over the world achieve and maintain optimal health by using reliable scientific evidence as a basis for their programs. Agricultural organizations, drug companies, food manufacturers, and other institutions do not fund the Wellness Forum. The website offers FAQs, podcasts, newsletters, and regularly updated information.

Index

visit us online . . .

www.jazzyvegetarian.com
For Recipes and More Information

About the Author

Laura Theodore is a radio host and television personality, vegan cook, sustainable lifestyle blogger, compassionate cookbook author, and award-winning jazz singer and actor. Laura has made guest appearances on ABC, NBC, CBS, USA, and public television. She has been featured in numerous newspapers and magazines, including the *New York Times*, *USA Today*, the *New York Daily News*, the *New York Post*, the *Dallas Morning News*, *People*, *JazzTimes*, *Variety*, and *Time*. Laura is the host, writer, and coproducer of the *Jazzy Vegetarian* television cooking show on public television. In addition, she hosts *Jazzy Vegetarian Radio*, a talk and music show that focuses on delicious, easy-to- prepare, plant-based recipes, earth-friendly entertaining tips, celebrity interviews, and upbeat music.

As an award-winning jazz singer and songwriter, Laura has recorded six solo albums, including *Tonight's the Night*, which received a *Musician* magazine award. Her 2009 release with the late, great Joe Beck, titled *Golden Earrings*, was selected to appear on the Fifty-Second Grammy Award list in the category "Best Jazz Vocal Album." Laura has toured throughout the country, performing at numerous major events, such as Night of 100 Stars, the Fire and Ice Ball, and the American Film Awards. In addition, she was host of the Manhattan Cable Network TV show *All That Jazz*, which ran for six years. On the acting side of things, Laura has appeared in over sixty plays and musicals, including Off-Broadway for two years in the hit show *Beehive*, which earned her a coveted Backstage Bistro Award. She was honored with the Denver Critics Drama Circle "Best Actress in a Musical" award for her starring role as Janis Joplin in the world-premiere production of the musical *Love, Janis*.

Her love of good food, compassion for animals, and enthusiasm for great music has created a joyous life path for Laura. She is proud to be the Jazzy Vegetarian!

Book Publishing Co.

Community owned since 1974

books that educate, inspire, and empower

To find your favorite vegetarian products online, visit:

www.healthy-eating.com

The 4 Ingredient Vegan
Maribeth Abrams
with Anne Dinshah
978-1-57067-232-3 $14.95

Becoming Vegan
Brenda Davis, RD,
Vesanto Melina, MS, RD
978-1-57067-103-6 $19.95

More Great Good Dairy-Free Desserts Naturally
Fran Costigan
978-1-57067-183-8 $19.95

Natural Vegan Kitchen
Christine Waltermyer
978-1-57067-245-3 $19.95

Speed Vegan
Alan Roettinger
978-1-57067-244-6 $19.95

Purchase these health titles and cookbooks from your local bookstore or natural food store, or you can buy them directly from:

Book Publishing Company • P.O. Box 99 • Summertown, TN 38483 • 1-800-695-2241

Please include $3.95 per book for shipping and handling.